*Studies of the New Testament
and Its World*

Edited by
JOHN BARCLAY
JOEL MARCUS
and
JOHN RICHES

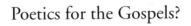

Poetics for the Gospels?

Poetics for the Gospels?

Rethinking Narrative Criticism

PETRI MERENLAHTI

T & T CLARK
A Continuum imprint
LONDON • NEW YORK

T&T CLARK LTD

A Continuum imprint

59 George Street
Edinburgh EH2 2LQ
Scotland

www.tandtclark.co.uk

370 Lexington Avenue
New York 10017–6503
USA

www.continuumbooks.com

First published 2002

ISBN 0 567 08851 0

0567042618

British Library Cataloguing-in-Publication Data
A catalogue record for this book is available from the British Library

Typeset by Waverley Typesetters, Galashiels
Printed and bound in Great Britain by MPG Books Ltd, Bodmin, Cornwall

Contents

Acknowledgments

This study is part of the research project *The Gospels as Stories* conducted in the Department of Biblical Studies at the University of Helsinki, Finland, during the years 1994–1999. I think warmly of my fellow members of that project, Raimo Hakola, Arto Järvinen, Outi Lehtipuu and Talvikki Mattila. It was a pleasure to work with them.

Among my team-mates, my greatest debt is to Raimo Hakola. During the six years in the project, we wrote so many papers together that I still occasionally find it hard to work on my own. Many ideas included in this book are originally his. I trust that he will feel free to use any of mine in the future, if he should find them useful.

Special thanks are due to my supervisor and the head of our project, Prof. Kari Syreeni, who currently holds the chair of New Testament studies at the University of Uppsala, Sweden. I was fortunate to have him as my mentor. I cherish the originality of his thought and his quenchless enthusiasm. His guidance always took place in an atmosphere of mutual respect and understanding.

In the fall of 1993, when I was starting my work, a scholarship negotiated by the Center of Foreign Affairs of the Evangelical Lutheran Church of Finland allowed me to spend three months as a Scholar-in-Residence at the Lutheran School of Theology at Chicago. There I came to know Prof. David Rhoads, whose encouragement, advice and support were to follow me throughout the conduct of this study. I will not forget the hearty welcome he gave to a young foreigner so critical towards his work. For me, he will always be a model of a dedicated scholar and a teacher who takes great responsibility for his students.

Among the staff of the Lutheran school, I would like to mention Margaret Koch-Gregersen, Director of International Student Affairs. Her care made it much easier for all of us, legal aliens, to adapt to life in the Windy City.

Later, Prof. Rhoads introduced me to the Literary Aspects of the Gospels and Acts Group of the Society of Biblical Literature. The sessions of this group proved both enjoyable and of great benefit to my work.

Other people whose help and encouragement were substantial include Prof. Heikki Räisänen (University of Helsinki) and Prof. Pekka Tammi (University of Tampere). One a world figure in New Testament studies, the other a distinguished expert in narratology, they kindly took the trouble of reading and commenting on my thesis at different stages in its making. Later I was helped by the comments made on the thesis by its examiner, Prof. Edgar V. McKnight (Furman University, South Carolina). Joan Nordlund did wonderful work in revising my English. If any mistakes remain, in terms of contents or in terms of language, they are due to my own negligence. Numerous friends and colleagues at the Department of Biblical Studies and elsewhere supported me in various ways. Whatever people say of lonely chambers in the ivory tower, scholarship is teamwork. *Heartfelt thanks to you all.*

I received financial support from the Research Center of the Evangelical Lutheran Church of Finland, the Finnish Cultural Foundation, the Finnish Graduate School of Theology (funded by the Academy of Finland) and the Research Unit for Early Jewish and Christian Culture and Literature sponsored by the Department of Biblical Studies at the University of Helsinki. I sincerely hope all parties were repaid for their investment in me.

The most important source of support and inspiration, however, was my family. No words can adequately express my gratitude to my parents Aila and Kalervo Virtanen, my lovely daughters Lahja and Saimi, and my beloved wife Anu. Not only was their helpfulness invaluable to my work, they also kept me from being absorbed by it completely. Ultimately, this may have rather delayed its completion – but frankly, I do not care.

Finally, I wish to thank John Riches for accepting my work in the present series. I should also acknowledge permission to reproduce some earlier material. Chapter 6 originally appeared in David Rhoads and Kari Syreeni (eds), *Characterization in the Gospels: Reconceiving Narrative Criticism* (JSNTSup 184, Sheffield: Sheffield Academic Press, 1999). Chapters 1, 2 and 4 contain parts of an earlier article, 'Reconceiving Narrative Criticism,' written by myself and Raimo Hakola and published in that same volume. Kari Syreeni's diagram 'The two axes and the three levels of analysis in a narrative text' was first presented in his essay,

'Peter as Character and Symbol in the Gospel of Matthew,' and is also included in *Characterization in the Gospels.* The diagram 'Vernon Robbins's socio-rhetorical model of textual communication' is taken from Vernon K. Robbins, *The Tapestry of Early Christian Discourse: Rhetoric, Society, and Ideology* (Routledge 1996). Biblical quotations, unless otherwise stated, are from the New Revised Standard Version.

Helsinki, March 2001   PETRI MERENLAHTI

1

Introduction

'[T]he real question is whether the poetic function of the gospels in the form that we now have them is a worthwhile subject for investigation.'

Mark Allan Powell (1990), 93.

In the Western tradition of literature and criticism, the term *poetics* refers to studies that concern the making of literary works of art. In these studies, the point of view may be either practical or theoretical. In the former case, the point at issue is *how to produce good literature*. This line of tradition is represented in handbooks on the subject, of which *Ars Poetica* by Horace (a poet himself) is a classic example. On the other hand, poetics is also a long-lived theoretical enterprise that is devoted to *critical analysis of aesthetic form*. Here the unrivalled classic is the *Poetics* of Aristotle (who, of course, was a philosopher).

In contemporary use, 'poetics' has mostly appeared in this latter, analytical sense. When proponents of literary-theoretical currents such as formalism and structuralism utilized structural analysis in order to produce a universal, 'scientific aesthetics' of literary art, it was natural for them to call this endeavor poetics. As a result, the term has been closely associated with these modern paradigms.

Lately, 'poetics' has increasingly become a catch-all term for theoretical commentary on cultural phenomena, 'a fashionable label for almost any kind of approach within literary and cultural studies.'[1] While its contents have turned vague, it seems to have won a new life as an attractive symbol. In the increasingly diversified field of critical practice, it can provide those who apply it with a sense of shared identity.

In New Testament studies, poetic influences have mostly been present in a formalist and structuralist mode. Accordingly, the term may first

[1] Mehtonen 1996, 12. Cf. Mehtonen 1993.

1

lead us to think of some highly technical expositions of the narrative grammar of the gospels and Acts.[2] In fact, we may also associate it with a particular methodological movement that displays an exclusive interest in the formal features of the gospels in their present form, namely *narrative criticism.*

From a wider perspective, a poetic interest is characteristic of an entire spectrum of 'new literary approaches' that have emerged in gospel studies, especially in the Anglophone world, during the last two decades or so.[3] Even though only few of these are overtly formalist, or display an interest in inherent properties of texts (some of them indeed deny the existence of texts altogether), they nevertheless share an explicitly 'literary' orientation. It is, actually, this very orientation that is supposed to make them something new and distinctive in the history of the discipline. In contrast with the ruling *historical-critical paradigm* of biblical studies, literary approaches would engage in an essentially different kind of investigation that views the gospels *as literature.*

But what is literature, and what makes an approach 'literary?' This has always been the crucial question for poetics. At present, it seems to be more acute than ever. We hear that a radical transformation of literary study is taking place, and that it involves 'a fundamental change in the conception of what constitutes the "literary".'[4] Critics now ask whether a category, literature, can be meaningfully constituted at all; and if so, whether it is worth much attention. Should we not rather focus on human culture(s) *in toto*, without making a distinction between high culture and popular culture, canonized aesthetic complexities and regular, everyday systems of meaning?

From Romanticism up until recently, what might be described as the 'traditional Western paradigm of literary study' commonly (although often somewhat unconsciously) assumed *an essence of literature* that was taken to be materialized in particular texts which comprised a *literary canon*. In *criticism, objectifiable features* of these texts were studied by means of *empirical methods* so as to grant them their due share of *literary value* – which was to confirm that the acceptance of these texts in the canon was well grounded. Among the criteria of qualification, *literary unity and coherence* stood out.[5]

[2] Here Funk 1988 might serve as a perfect example.
[3] See e.g. Moore 1989; Malbon and McKnight (eds) 1994; Porter 1995.
[4] Levine 1994, 1.
[5] See Easthope 1991, esp. pp. 9–12; cf. Felperin 1985, 24.

When narrative critics first advocated a literary approach to the New Testament, they essentially subscribed to this traditional literary paradigm. They made a programmatic claim that 'a literary study of [a gospel's] formal features suggests that the author succeeded in creating a unified narrative.'[6] In other words, narrative critics viewed objectifiable unity as a core value and applied an empirical method to discover that unity in the narratives of the gospels. Once they had found a sufficient amount of unity to enable them to conclude that the gospels are of literary value, they could also maintain that literary analysis of the gospels was a meaningful task.

As was to be expected, some scholarly opponents of the narrative critics soon accused them of 'uncritical admiration of the literary accomplishments of the evangelists.'[7] The debate concerned, essentially, one single question, even if it had three sides:

Are the gospels (1) unified enough to (2) be valued as literature, which would justify (3) a 'literary' approach?

As it turns out, not only was the affirmative answer given to this question in narrative criticism open to doubt, but the question itself, and the underlying literary paradigm, was also problematic. Unity, not to mention 'sufficient unity,' is not a matter of objective observation. Rather, it is a particular way of perceiving and evaluating texts. In texts that are taken to be of literary value, unity (or any other sign of artistic merit) is typically found by means of *interpretation*. The means of interpretation, however, are contingent – that is, they change from one historical and cultural context to another – and the same holds true for every choice of criteria of literary value, including the criterion of unity. This means that, ultimately, the justification of any canon of literature, on the basis of whatever observable features, only rests upon a hegemony of interpretation maintained by a community of elect critics.[8]

Once critics became aware of this (and such awareness has indeed been widespread among critics for some time), efforts to replace contingent, axiological approaches – interpretation and criticism – with poetics as value-free *description* followed. These efforts could claim an

[6] Rhoads and Michie 1982, 3.
[7] Räisänen 1995, 128.
[8] This is the core of the criticism offered by Marxism, structuralism, and deconstruction alike against traditional literary studies; see e.g. Felperin 1985, 10–11.

ancient tradition. Aristotle himself, while as critic being interested in what makes a dramatic plot a good one, nevertheless did not consider the value of the text as the criterion of its literariness. His poetics was concerned with *mimesis*: Empedocles, although he may write well in verse, is not a poet but a scientist (*Poetics* 1447b); even if put into verse, the writings of Herodotus would still belong to the genre of history (*Poetics* 1451b). And, of course, even a very bad play is a play none the less. Literature should be regarded not as the perceived value, but as the essential nature of certain types of text.

For a while, people were quite optimistic that they might actually objectify this literary nature manifest in certain types of texts. Once this had taken place, poetics would have made literary studies empirical science (which criticism, not to mention interpretation, was not). In the first half of the 20th century, the Russian Formalists and the Prague linguists were still confident that they could define 'literariness' (*literaturnost*) as a linguistic feature. Later, the structuralists and the Marxists energetically looked elsewhere for viable grounds for objective analysis of literary texts. Unfortunately, these attempts have fared rather badly in the long run. From whatever aspect of textuality we may look, whether it be language, form, semiosis, ideology, gender, institution, fantasy and the unconscious or subject position, no *terra firma* for objective poetics – literature as such – seems to have been found.

Here, then, we face the pertinent question that the present study aims to answer: if the basis for a traditional 'literary approach,' as well as for an objective theory of poetics, is lost, can 'a poetics for the gospels' still exist as a meaningful enterprise, and if the answer is yes, on what conditions can this take place?

Some initial hope may be found in the fact that, no matter how terminally ill it is in theory, in practice literature is alive and well. Literary canons and literary institutions happily exist as historical and cultural (or subcultural) phenomena, even if they may now come in somewhat more particular and diffuse forms than before. People continue to engage in what they understand as producing literature, and the output of this activity is studied in departments of English (or Russian, or Czech, or French), alongside other cultural systems of signs (film, folklore, advertising, varieties of social discourse) that no doubt deserve their share of critical attention, too. Even though critics have what seem to be permanent difficulties in *defining*, in terms of a comprehensive theory, any difference between poetic and other forms of language, they quite successfully *demonstrate* that difference by writing not literature but *about* literature. Against all odds, literature survives, 'not as an essence, an entity, a thing, but as a process, a function.'[9]

In all probability, then, poetics will also have a chance of survival. In the practical, handbook context, this is actually quite obvious. Creative writers will hardly give up assuming high standards and then putting effort into attaining them. In George Steiner's words, 'structure is itself interpretation and composition is criticism,' so that 'in painting and sculpture, as in literature, the focused light of both interpretation (the hermeneutic) and valuation (the critical-normative) lies in the work itself.'[10]

Poetics is also likely to persist in a secondary, critical role – even if not exactly in the way in which it used to exist. Stripped of claims of objectivity and universality, it will have to become an historically and ideologically sensitive discipline. It will need to adapt to the fact that perceptions of literary form, function, meaning and value are not fixed for all time, but mutate and develop from one time and culture to another;[11] and that, far from being neutral, these perceptions are integrally connected with ways of perceiving reality that reflect particular interests in human societies.[12]

Significantly, this need not lead to reductionism, subjectivism or absolute relativism. It will not be necessary to join the Marxists and assume that textual features are *products* of historical and ideological conditions, or that they return to them fully in one way or another. Nor will it be necessary to affirm the memorable saying of Harold Bloom and conclude that, in the end, there are no texts, only readings.[13] While it would, of course, be impossible ever to know any texts 'as they are,' that is, as *unread*, this will in no way prevent contextual readings from informing us about qualities of texts. The fact that we read a poem differently than we read the telephone book has to do not only with prevalent reading conventions in particular interpretive communities, but also with the different textual features of the documents in question.

[9] Easthope 1991, 53; cf. Felperin 1985, 45.
[10] Steiner 1989, 21, 17.
[11] Cf. e.g. Earl Miner's recent intercultural approach (Miner 1990).
[12] Cf. Eagleton 1983, 16. For a program of *sociological poetics*, see Swingewood 1986.
[13] Bloom 1979, 7.

This is not to say that all kinds of readings are not *possible* for all kinds of text; critics such as Stanley Fish have, rather convincingly, demonstrated that practically anything *can* be read as literature.[14] Rather, the idea is that, in terms of textuality, not all kinds of text are the same. Today, one can indeed take a selection from the telephone book (or, as Tzara actually dreamed of doing, a selection from the evening paper) and read it as a poem, but this is because *current historical standards of literature* allow 'a poem' to have a practically infinite variety of textual features.

Accordingly, each gospel narrative, while it can only acquire meaning(s) and value in variable historical and ideological contexts, also has a textual identity of its own. Textually, the gospel of Luke is not just the same as the gospel of Mark. Each of these two narratives independently transforms the form currently known as 'gospel' and makes it something more than it was before – as some scholars might say, even shifts it from one genre to another.

Thus, poetics for the gospels remains possible – but it will necessarily be historical, not objective poetics. Whether it is Luke or Mark that is considered more 'literary' will change – and indeed has changed – depending on currents in cultural history. In antiquity, people could appreciate Luke's more constant rhetorical and moral patterns. In modern times, Mark's 'popular realism' and 'savage polyvalence' have greater appeal.

At first glance, this might seem to make a poetic approach to the gospels simply a(nother) project within the field of comparative literary history. Such a fusion of interests has indeed been in the ascendancy in recent gospel studies. Focusing on the gospels in their original literary environment, a number of studies have investigated their salient features and looked for analogies to other ancient Greco-Roman writings. While many of these investigations are primarily concerned with the question of the genre of the New Testament gospels,[15] others sustain a more directly poetic or literary-historical interest.[16] Some consider the later literary or cultural reception of the Bible in some distinct historical era or/and by some distinct cultural group, offering 'imaginative

---

[14] See Fish 1980.
[15] Thus e.g. Burridge 1992.
[16] See e.g. Bilezikian 1977; Tolbert 1989; Shiner 1995; Hock, Chance and Perkins (eds) 1999.

reconstructions' of how a particular reader might once have viewed the text.[17]

Yet there is more at stake than just making a traditionally ahistorical study properly historical. Even as re-defined and relativized in historical terms, poetics in a formalist sense remains a conceptualization, an abstract quantity, a human-made fiction. In reality, it does not only concern the ideologically innocent, functional question 'How does the text work?' The conception, production and reception of symbolic, meaningful forms are rather thoroughly invaded by an essentially ideological element, namely the conception, production and reception of meaning as a social and ideological construct. One cannot imagine, create or perceive a symbolic form without being informed of its nature as a symbolic form. The source of this information is, as coined by scholars of the sociology of knowledge, one's *symbolic universe*, that socially conditioned, ideologically constructed interpretive limbo where human experience of reality lingers for the short moment it takes for it to make sense.[18]

Consequently, the utter historicity of poetics also means that poetics itself, as a critical discipline, will have to become *hermeneutical*. It will be concerned with how poetic forms function in texts, and with what conditions shape human understanding of poetic forms in different places and at different times.[19]

While this insight has (under labels such as 'new historicism' and cultural studies) won extensive popularity recently, it is essentially not new. In different formulations, it can be found in the thoughts of several prominent 20th-century theorists. In his early 'translinguistics,' Mikhail Bakhtin conceived of the text as a dialogue of different voices emerging from different social and ideological locations. In a system of

---

[17] Thus e.g. Erickson 1997.

[18] Cf. Syreeni 1995, 328; on the concept of the symbolic universe, see Berger and Luckmann 1967.

[19] Stephen Greenblatt has coined the term *cultural poetics*. The concerns of cultural poetics include 'how collective beliefs and experiences were shaped, moved from one medium to another, concentrated in manageable aesthetic form, offered for consumption [and] how the boundaries were marked between cultural practices understood to be art forms and other, contiguous, forms of expression' (Greenblatt 1988, 5). The hermeneutic tone of Greenblatt's project (which has subsequently become constitutive to a larger movement known as 'new historicism') is also to be seen in his call to accept the impossibility of leaving behind one's own situation, of not having the questions we ask of our study material shaped by the questions we ask of ourselves (Greenblatt 1980, 4–5).

Rezeptionsästhetik, Hans Robert Jauss brought together the different historical traditions of formalist poetics and philosophical hermeneutics. Michel Foucault shed light on the history of the human subject as the maker of his or her reality in critical projects named 'archaeological' and 'genealogical.' Insisting that, as processes of signification, texts are properly written by people who read them, Roland Barthes concluded that 'in the text, only the reader speaks.'[20]

Moreover – and this is especially interesting from the point of view of the present study – a number of critics suggest that the inescapable interdependence of poetic and ideological aspects is particularly striking in the case of biblical texts. Thus Paul Ricoeur, for example, contends that the gospels par excellance are 'interpretative narratives,' that is, 'narratives in which the ideological interpretation these narratives wish to convey is not superimposed on the narrative by the narrator but is, instead, incorporated into the very strategy of narrative,' so that the result is an 'indissociable union of the kerygmatic and the narrative aspects.'[21]

As I see it, the word 'indissociable' here does *not* mean that the two aspects actually *merge.* Rather, it implies that in certain cases one aspect has so penetratingly assumed the image of the other that an innocent reader cannot necessarily tell them apart. Thus, in modernist poetry where form itself would seem to be the only content, an innocent reader may come to think that *form itself, as content,* might not convey an ideological interpretation. Correspondingly, in the somewhat opposite case of biblical narratives in which the content is so obviously ideological, an innocent reader may not realize that their very *form* might incorporate an ideological interpretation *as well.*

Once innocence is lost, however, and the presence of ideological interpretation is discovered in the aesthetic form, poetics becomes an irrevocably serious business. What formerly might have appeared as casual delight in a play on words or a symphony of language has now turned into a grave responsibility to be critical, even suspicious. Aware that the formal configuration of the text is not neutral, but rather

---

[20] Barthes 1974 (1970), 151.

[21] Ricoeur 1990, 237, 239. In analyses of the Hebrew Bible, similar ideas have been proposed by Robert Alter (1981) and Meir Sternberg (1987). Also, as narrative-critical analyses typically emphasize the nature of the gospels as *'narrative christologies'* (Tannehill 1979), they thereby suggest that poetic and hermeneutic elements of analysis are present simultaneously.

associated with meanings made by people in societies – more concretely, structures of power and control – the critic can no longer avoid taking a stand. Exposing and questioning – or, alternatively, naturalizing – these structures becomes a part of the critic's lot. *Sachkritik* has come to involve the form of biblical texts as well as their content.

*

Having established that historical poetics focuses on poetic forms and, inalienably, on their historical, cultural and ideological constitution, we still need to define what exactly we mean by poetic form in the case of the gospels. Does poetic analysis limit itself to identification of textual or narrative strategies and exclude all questions concerning the nature or value of those strategies as literary expression? This, I think, is a valid approach (although it might be more accurate to describe it as narratological rather than poetic). Another, slightly more explicit way of claiming a poetic perspective is to say that we will assess the textual meaning and aesthetic impact of the gospels on the basis of their nature as *composed artefacts*. In that case, poetic interest is justified by virtue of the fact that the gospels comprise *poiesis*, or *narrative fiction*, in the restricted sense that their making involves selection, composition, rhetoric and imagination.[22] While this may be a rather broad definition of literary art, it seems to be as far as we can go in closing up the scope of poetics, if it is still to include the gospels as its subjects of study.

What we cannot license in particular are readings that view the gospels as *fictional narratives* which (as Aristotle put it) aim to tell not what actually happened, but what could happen (*Poetics* 1451a). Indeed, I do not think that Aristotle would have regarded the gospels as poetic works. For him, poetics was about *mimesis* – that is, representation or '*simulation* of imaginary actions and events.'[23] For the gospels – as well as for (other) biographical or historical works – rhetoric would have been a more appropriate context.

Certainly, the concepts of mimesis and representation have become utterly problematic since Aristotle's days. According to Derrida's famous dictum (to summon up the one modern luminary who perhaps might have a chance to match something of Aristotle's radiance), 'there is

---

[22] Cf. Rhoads 1982, 413; Tolbert 1989, 30.
[23] Genette 1993, 7.

nothing outside the text;' what is re-presented never was a real presence at all, but rather an(other) occasion of textuality, construction, invention. Language does not represent but rather replaces the in itself unattainable reality. Sensitive to this trauma of absence, postmodern writing typically blurs the difference between fiction and non-fiction.

At the same time, *pragmatic* differences between fictional and non-fictional texts remain evident. The textual features of a novel and a newscast, a poem and a weather report, a tragedy and a gospel are understood differently. This is in spite of the fact that there are no definite formal differences between non-fictional or 'factual' and fictional discourse.[24] Nor need factual discourses be true in order to remain factual, or fictive totally invented to count as fiction. What matters is not the *truth value*, but the (explicit or implicit) *truth claim* that identifies the aim of the work for practical purposes.[25]

That it remains possible to read factual discourse as fiction, and vice versa, is, of course, a fact – but the more serious this kind of reading is intended to be, the more likely it will give results that are devastating in one way or another. Gospel studies are no exception here, but rather a typical case.

If misinterpretations were only technical, the amount of damage done would be rather small. However, to say that, for example, the narrative of the Luke–Acts has an 'unreliable narrator'[26] (a technical category applicable to texts of fiction), not only produces an anachronistic reading of an ancient narrative, but involves a profound misunderstanding of the nature of gospel literature as narrative communication.[27] The crucial question here concerns the *responsibility* of the evangelist for the good news he is telling.

Fiction is a game of make-believe.[28] According to the rules of this game, the narrator is part of the fictive world. He or she (or it) does not represent the author. If the author is brought to court for trial because of the commitments and beliefs represented by the narrator, we (or at

[24] Cf. Tammi 1995, 371.
[25] Cf. Sternberg 1985, 25.
[26] This term, coined by Wayne C. Booth (1983 [1961], 158–159) refers to a narrator whose norms and behavior are not in accordance with the norms of the work.
[27] Such a reading is *de facto* proposed by James Dawsey (1986), although he fails to mention the term 'unreliable narrator' explicitly. The anachronism is aptly noted by Moore 1989, 33.
[28] Thus Walton 1990, 11 and *passim*; see also Currie 1990, 18–21; Calinescu 1993, 188.

least most of us) would say this is due to a severe misconception concerning the relationship between fiction and reality.[29]

In factual narratives, on the other hand, 'the author assumes full responsibility for the assertions of his narrative, and consequently grants no shred of autonomy to any narrator whatsoever.'[30] A doctor is held responsible for her diagnosis, a journalist for his news report and an evangelist for the gospel he proclaims. The positive side is that the doctor can require that the patient will follow her orders, the journalist may hope that his report gives people reason to act and the evangelist may expect his audience to observe Jesus' teaching and example.

It is significant that analyses which mistakenly read the gospels as fictional narratives often relate to issues such as anti-Semitism on which we might think a modern reader could actually call the evangelists to trial. The typical argument runs as follows. The portrayal of (some or all) Jews as villainous in a given gospel is seen as a rhetorical device used by the narrator to highlight the battle between good and evil that takes place *inside the narrative*. As such, it is in no way intended to say anything about any real historical people in the world *outside the story*. Consequently, the evangelist should not be held responsible for fostering anti-Semitism.[31]

The trouble with this argument is that if it can be extended to concern some non-fictional texts, there is no reason why it should not be extended to concern all non-fictional texts of similar type – including pieces of openly racist discourse. One could then, say, make a documentary film to fight crime by showing how foolish criminals are and using certain ethnic groups as historical examples, *just for the sake of argument*. On the other hand, if the argument only holds good for fiction – on the basis that fiction assumes a relative disinterest with respect to the real world – then we will need to go all the way and conclude that, as far as their poetic function is concerned, the gospels make no claims that concern actual history. That is to say, they can represent historical people, places or events, but they are in no way committed to doing so; their narrators may endorse certain ideological views, but these are

[29] Tammi 1995, 381.
[30] Genette 1993, 70; similarly Cohn 1990, 792: 'the reader of a nonfictional narrative understands it to have a stable uni-vocal origin, that its narrator is identical to a real person.'
[31] See e.g. Powell 1990, 66–67. For further discussion, see pp. 122–123 below.

11

not meant to be accepted by the audience. This, however, is hardly the case.

In practice, the difference between fiction and non-fiction matters, at least in the analysis of the gospels.[32] A poetic approach that wishes to view the gospels as literature can only operate under such broad definitions of poetics and literature that include such non-fictional, ideologically committed narratives as the gospels. This inclusion may be due to a neutral perspective that focuses on all kinds of narrative discourse, regardless of medium, fictionality or value.[33] Or it could result from a restricted historical and cultural point of view that relates 'the art of the gospel narratives' explicitly to some particular set of literary virtues historically applied not only to fiction but to history, auto-biography, the essay and the like, the gospel included.

*

The present work, a series of critical essays, adheres to and further explicates the program of historical poetics briefly outlined above. In Part I, I will describe the origins and nature of narrative criticism in gospel studies; how this particular methodological movement, in a manner typical of 'traditional Western literary study,' fused together questions concerning the narrative unity of the gospels, their literary value, and the appropriateness of a literary approach (poetics). I will then take a brief look at aspects of the modern literary treatment of Mark, thus seeking to create a basis for understanding the gospel's observed literary value as a variable, historical quantity. I will proceed to argue that readings which claim to be 'purely poetic' (and thus ideologically neutral) take too much for granted. Writings and readings each come from a place that is somewhere else than in the world of the story. This is especially true of narratives such as the gospels that were composed for the purposes of ideological interpretation.

Part II consists of a series of analyses that focus on the intertwined nature of the poetic and hermeneutic aspects of the gospels, as well as on the complex interrelationships of text, history and ideology. Giving

---

[32] For a more detailed treatment of the difference between fictional and non-fictional narratives, and the difference this makes in gospel studies, see Merenlahti and Hakola 1999, 33–43.

[33] This was the original starting point of structuralist narratology, as outlined in e.g. Todorov 1969, Barthes 1966 and Bal 1977 (cf. Tammi 1992, 172; Tammi 1995, 369).

a bow of respect to a long-lived tradition, I will center on three *loci classici* of narrative theory, that is, narrative rhetoric, characterization and plot. Classic as these aspects are, each of them also has a significant as well as a rather specific relationship with ideology. In the case of narrative rhetoric, this is more than obvious, rhetoric being the means by which the narrator is seen to impose his or her ideological position upon the narratee. Characterization, in turn, has become a great crux in recent discussions concerning textual manifestations of ideology. On the one hand, because individuality *per definitionem* implies deviation, representation of individuality can be viewed as potentially subversive, a challenge to hegemonies that seek to retain the *status quo*. On the other hand, representation of individuality has also been regarded as bourgeois and reactionary *per se*, because it necessarily implies a false perception of reality as a matter of personal choice rather than as a matter of historico-economic determinacy. Finally, plot – the material shaping-force of narrative – properly embodies the clear and present ideological implications of every narrative's nature as selective fiction. For can there ever be a claim more fabulous (in the very literal sense of the word) or more profoundly ideological than to say that, distilled from that initially diffuse and nameless event we call reality, it is a particular story that matters and makes sense?

In Part III, I seek to relocate the position of poetics as part of some broader interpretive framework in current New Testament study. Evidently, the traditional historical-critical paradigm as such has been shown to be unable to cope with the textual particularity of the gospel narratives; in this respect, narrative criticism has emerged as a necessary antithesis. On the other hand, due to its ahistorical nature and blindness to ideology, the traditional literary paradigm to which narrative criticism initially subscribed has proven to be inadequate as well. What is required is a new type of paradigm that properly deals with the blind spots of its predecessors. I will argue that for historical poetics of the gospels to be consonant with such a paradigm might mean one of two things.

First, we may try to attain a radically more comprehensive and, above all, hermeneutically better-informed model of textual interpretation than previous ones. This would allow us to perceive formal features of texts as objectifications of variable historical, social and cultural experience. Projects that display a conscious move in this direction are already present in the field of New Testament studies.

A second alternative would be to engage in an inherently historically-conditioned primary encounter with the text rather than in secondary description of historical experience. In simple terms, this refers to an individual critic's or interpreter's own personal response, for which each critic or interpreter – a historical person and an ideological being – would be held fully accountable. Besides this, I also have a more systematic praxis in mind, namely the use of what might be called *deliberate interpretive fictions*, or *instrumental metaphors*. With no 'real' explanatory power, these would convey an intuition, a hunch, a sense of meaningfulness present in (or, strictly speaking, absent from) the text.

What is significant is that these two options – the use of secondary descriptive models on the one hand and the use of instrumental metaphors on the other – are not entirely mutually exclusive. Every descriptive model is human-made and metaphoric in the sense that it lacks immediate access to the phenomena it seeks to investigate. Strictly speaking, it does not describe but *narrates*. Certainly, this alone does not make all approaches the same. The amount of relative descriptive power available varies significantly from one reading to another (which makes a serious methodological reform necessary). Yet in every case that power is *relative*.

Thus, a peculiar condition of *complementarity* seems to prevail between aspects of secondary description and primary response, relative truth and conjuring fiction, in poetics. All poetics has two natures: one as an authoritative metanarrative with a sublime will to exert power, the other as an exuberant work of literary imagination.

Part I

2

Are the Gospels Unified Narratives?

The Origins of Narrative Criticism

Narrative analysis of the gospels originated in the late 1970s and early 1980s. At that time, a number of New Testament scholars sought a holistic approach that would give value to the compositional unity of the gospel narratives. Narratological models, which at the time represented the *avant-garde* in literary studies, provided these scholars with serviceable methodological tools.[1] What resulted was *narrative criticism*, a movement that aims at including formal analysis of narrative as a new member in the family of exegetical methods.

Much of the work that led to the development of narrative criticism was undertaken in the Markan Seminar of the Society of Biblical Literature, chaired first by Norman Perrin, and then by Werner Kelber, between 1971 and 1980.[2] During the final year of that seminar, David Rhoads delivered a programmatic paper called 'Narrative Criticism and the Gospel of Mark.'[3] In this paper he coined the term 'narrative criticism' to describe particular investigative areas of contemporary literary criticism as applied to the study of the gospels. More precisely, the new approach comprised 'investigating the formal features of narrative in

---

[1] The term 'narratology' was first proposed by Tzvetan Todorov (Todorov 1969, 10). Originally, the term referred to the structuralist study of narrative. Later on, it came to be used in a broader sense, with reference to formal theories of narrative (and narrativity) in general. Such theories flourished especially in the late 1970s and early 1980s, when several comprehensive narratological syntheses appeared (Genette 1980 [1972]; Chatman 1978; Stanzel 1986 [1979]; Bal 1985 [1980]; Prince 1982; Rimmon-Kenan 1983; Martin 1986).

[2] Thomas Boomershine, Joanna Dewey, Robert Fowler, Norman Petersen, Robert Tannehill, and Mary Ann Tolbert were among the seminar members who were 'particularly influential in the development of the new discipline' (Powell 1990, 110 n. 24).

[3] The paper was published two years later in the *Journal of the American Academy of Religion* (Rhoads 1982).

the texts of the gospels, features which include aspects of the story-world of the narrative and the rhetorical techniques employed to tell the story.'[4]

According to Rhoads, the new, literary approach involved for him, as a New Testament scholar, two shifts of perspective. The first shift moved *toward a more holistic point of view,* that is, *an emphasis on the unity of the narrative.* Whereas traditional source-, form-, and redaction-critical methods had cut the gospels into small pieces of tradition and redaction, narrative criticism focused on them as *complete literary wholes.* The second shift involved moving away from the historical, or theological questions concerning the gospel's author or audience toward *an exclusively text-oriented approach* that 'looks at the closed universe of the story-world.'[5] The value of such investigation seemed for Rhoads 'patently clear:' 'After all, Mark is a story, *and a very good one at that.*'[6]

Since that time, the essence of narrative criticism has been defined several times both within the movement and outside it.[7] On the other hand, the fundamentals of the approach were already present in Rhoads' concise program as paraphrased above. These include:

(1) A view of narrative as a two-level structure where one can distinguish between aspects of form and content, the 'how' and the 'what' of narrative.

This view is truly a classic one; it originates in Aristotle, was taken up by the Russian Formalists, and became constitutive of a number of narratological theories. Rhoads had adopted it from the American critic Seymour Chatman, whose work has since remained perhaps the most

---

[4] Rhoads 1982, 411–412.

[5] Rhoads 1982, 413. Rhoads' notion of two shifts illustrates the differences between the old and the new approaches. On the other hand, we can also identify significant elements of continuity. According to Norman Perrin, it was more or less inevitable that redaction criticism should develop into 'genuine literary criticism' (Perrin 1976, 120). More recently, Mary Ann Tolbert has described redaction criticism as a 'transitional discipline' that 'has led directly to the beginnings of more broadly conceived literary examinations of the gospels on one hand and to more sophisticated sociological analyses of the gospels' communities on the other' (Tolbert 1989, 23). Indeed, both a literary point of view – that is, an idea of the gospels as composed artefacts – and a sociological point of view – an idea that communal factors explain editorial decisions made by the evangelists and are the proper source of their 'theology' – were, and continue to be, an integral part of redaction criticism (Cf. Donahue 1994). In all probability, the future of New Testament studies will witness an increasing reintegration of these two points of view. I will return to this in the third part of this book.

[6] Rhoads 1982, 412 (emphasis added).

[7] See e.g. Moore 1989, 1–68; Powell 1990; Malbon 1992; Moore 1994, 65–81.

important single source of inspiration for narrative critics of the New Testament.[8]

In addition to providing the basic narratological toolbox, Rhoads' program necessitated a number of more general background assumptions, such as:

(2) an idea of a distinct *literary* approach that investigates the gospels *as literature*;

(3) a view of the text as a closed literary object whose form can be observed empirically;

(4) a belief that formal analysis can reveal the text's literary value which, in turn, is based on the inherent unity of the text.

Together, these assumptions form a circle. To prove, empirically, that the gospels are unified narratives is to prove that they qualify as literature, which will legitimate a literary approach.

While the methodological basis of narrative criticism is essentially narratological, these more general assumptions – the 'literary paradigm' of which narrative criticism apparently is a part – show traces that go in another direction. That is, they smack of *American formalism*, also known as the New Criticism.[9]

New-critical influences came to narrative criticism in several different ways. First, some earlier experiments using a 'literary approach' to the New Testament had been drawing extensively (and, in contrast to the early narrative criticism, explicitly) on the New Criticism; in a sense, narrative criticism went along a beaten path.[10] Second, many essentials of the new-critical program had continued to exert a covert influence

[8] The following lines with which Jack Dean Kingsbury presented his *Matthew as Story* (1986) showed in a nutshell what much of the future of narrative criticism was to be like: 'One literary theorist, Seymour Chatman, has provided a useful outline for discussing the constituent parts of narrative, and David Rhoads has shown us with what profit this outline can be employed in investigating a gospel such as that of Mark. The present investigation of Matthew's gospel will also draw from Chatman's outline, and supplement it as well with the work of others.' (Kingsbury 1986, 1; cf. Moore 1989, 51.)

[9] Stephen D. Moore was among the first to take notice of this. See Moore 1989, 9–12; Moore 1994, 68; cf. The Bible and Culture Collective 1995, 85–87. Soon enough, the debt owed by narrative criticism to New Criticism became acknowledged by narrative critics themselves. See e.g. Malbon 1992, 24–26.

[10] Such experiments include the highly significant work of the Parables Seminar of the Society of Biblical Literature, involving scholars such as William Beardslee, John Dominic Crossan, Robert Funk, James Robinson, Robert Tannehill, Dan Via, and (last but certainly not least) Amos Wilder, and leading to the founding of the periodical *Semeia* in 1973.

on the American academic scene long after the methodological school itself had become *passé*. With little or no explicit interest in theory, standard literary studies – 'practical criticism' – implicitly subscribed to the new-critical program and the modernist canon that went with it. On the theoretical side, emergent newer currents engaged in polemics with practical criticism – but simultaneously remained dependent on a very similar concept of literary institution to the one that once had made New Criticism and practical criticism seem legitimate.

Significantly, the literary-critical paradigm that became crystallized in America as New Criticism is, actually, part of a wider phenomenon. As such, its roots go all the way back to the Romanticism that first gave 'literature' an autonomous role in performances of the human spirit. Ever since, a basically similar essentialism has remained characteristic of the Western literary-critical institution, even until the great theory wars (Martin Kreiswirth's term) of the last two decades.[11]

As could be expected, the same traditional, essentialist conception of literature also colored assessments made of the literary nature of the gospels by historical-critical scholars well before the emergence of narrative criticism. In suggesting that the gospels should not be regarded as literature due to their essentially popular nature (the gospels as *Volksliteratur*, or *Kleinliteratur*) and disembodied structure, historical-critical scholarship apparently

(1) assumed there was a canon of literature;

(2) distinguished between literature and popular culture;

(3) conceived that literary texts are unified;

(4) believed that one can give objective judgments on the unity of texts.

From these starting-points, narrative criticism might have produced an essentially new-critical method of New Testament study merely by producing a direct antithesis of whatever previous scholarship had once said against the literary nature of the gospel narratives. Incidentally, this is very much what happened.

The emergence of narrative criticism in the Markan Seminar of the Society of Biblical Literature properly belongs in the broader framework of the so-called 'creativity debate' that focused on the role of Mark the evangelist in the making of his gospel – whether the earliest gospel was

---

[11] Cf. Felperin 1985, 14.

to be considered the work of a genuine artist or rather a clumsily edited collection of diverse traditional material. This debate was hotly contested and, eventually, resulted in a split within Markan studies.[12] It was very much in the context of this debate that Rhoads and others first made the claim that 'a literary study of [Mark's] formal features suggests that the author succeeded in creating a unified narrative.' In this assessment, the unity of the gospels, their literary value, and the usefulness of a literary approach joined into an indissociable triune alliance. Correspondingly, the disagreement between proponents of narrative criticism and their critics came to be, mostly, a disagreement on whether the gospels are unified narratives, *ergo* successful narratives, *ergo* literature.

The Gospel Clockwork

To make its case, narrative criticism applied narratology and assumed the task of exposing, systematically, how a gospel works as narrative. Narrative critics labored to present the text's formal narrative structure, that is, the narrative mechanics according to which the gospel was assumed to function as a structure of communication between the author and the reader. At first, some individual facets of these mechanics were investigated in topical studies.[13] The real breakthrough in the new approach, however, came with the appearance of two monograph studies, David Rhoads' and Donald Michie's *Mark as Story: An Introduction to the Narrative of a Gospel* (1982), and R. Alan Culpepper's *Anatomy of the Fourth Gospel: A Study in Literary Design* (1983). Both works aimed at presenting a comprehensive *descriptive poetics* of a gospel. Both were also heavily influenced by one particular narratological synthesis of the time, namely Seymour Chatman's 1978 *Story and Discourse: Narrative Structure in Fiction and Film*.

Concise, elegantly written, and easy to read, *Mark as Story* in particular became a highly influential book. Rhoads' and Michie's readings of Mark's narrative became noted for their insight and inspiration. As to the success of Mark's work, Rhoads and Michie concluded that literary analysis revealed the evangelist to be a masterly storyteller in full command of his material:

---

[12] On the debate, see Räisänen 1990, 1–37.
[13] These include e.g. Boomershine 1974, Tannehill 1977, and Petersen 1978a.

[T]he writer [of Mark] has told the story in such a way as to have certain effects on the reader . . . The author has used sophisticated literary techniques, developed the characters and the conflicts and built suspense with deliberateness, telling the story in such way as to generate certain emotions and insights in the reader.[14]

Later, the great majority of narrative-critical studies would assume a similar view.

It is notable that Rhoads and Michie were talking about the *author* of Mark at this point. In effect, they were discussing with the form critics and the redaction critics the very same questions those critics had asked once before: How did the evangelist work? Was he a creative author in charge of his work, or rather a passive collector of traditional material?

In terms of the narratological method, this may appear somewhat problematic. As a descriptive theory of narrative, narratology will not tell us anything about the evangelist's actual role in the creation of his work. Nor does narratological analysis as such warrant any evaluative statements concerning the literary success, or failure, of a particular narrative work. Properly, narratology confines itself to describing what the *narrator* (the one who tells the story, *as inscribed in the text*) does in a text (that may or may not be considered 'literary'). The concepts of *implied author* and *implied reader* refer to the author and the audience *presupposed within the text itself*. If the critic still wants to know what *the real author(s)* has (have) done (*with deliberateness*) with their material, it is (back) to the historical, 'extrinsic' methods he or she must turn.[15] And if the critic wants to make an assessment of the literary value of the work in question, he or she will need some additional criteria in order to do so.

---

[14] Rhoads and Michie 1982, 1. Culpepper's assessment of John's success is a more cautious one: 'The gospel of John is therefore more unified and coherent than has often been thought because its unity is not found primarily in plot development, which as we have seen is rather episodic, or in the progression of action from scene to scene. It consists instead in the effect it achieves through thematic development, the spectrum of characters, and the implicit commentary conveyed through irony and symbolism. In other words, the unity of the "spiritual gospel" is more evident in the subtle elements of its narrative structure than in the obvious ones. The eagle soars when it reaches for the sublime and the subtle, but it is clumsy when it has to walk through some of the ordinary elements of a narrative.' (Culpepper 1983, 234.)

[15] Cf. Moore 1989, 12. Indeed, there is more at stake here than mere terminological purism. To avoid circular arguments, it is essential that the question 'What does the narrator do in the text?' is not confused with the question 'What has the author/composer done?'

On the other hand, narrative criticism never was a pure, straight-forward application of narratology to the texts of the gospels. While narrative critics drew upon narratological (and later, reader-oriented) models to view the texts as narrative communication, their interests were not limited to descriptive poetics or to the process of narrative communication as such. Essentially, they were taking part in the redaction-critical creativity debate and presenting arguments for the literary value of the gospels (and, consequently, for the validity of their own approach.)[16]

Not that Rhoads' and Michie's conclusion did not make sense. In its simple persuasiveness it was reminiscent of the classical deist argument of a person who finds a clock and assumes that someone must once have made it. In this case, as applied to Mark, it went as follows: if a narrative-critical analysis is able to demonstrate consistent literary or artistic patterns going through the whole of the gospel, there must once have been someone capable of putting them there. It takes a qualified artist to create a work with integrity.

But Are the Gospels Unified Narratives?

Since the publication of *Mark as Story* and *The Anatomy of the Fourth Gospel,* numerous narrative-critical studies on the four gospels and the Acts of the Apostles have appeared. Without exception, they all strongly emphasize the narrative unity of these works. Again and again the reader learns that the gospels are

> of remarkably whole cloth: the narrator maintains a unifying point of view; the standards of judgment are uniform; the plot is coherent; the characters are introduced and developed with consistency; stylistic patterns persist through the story; and there is a satisfying overall rhetorical effect.[17]

By any standards, a strong emphasis on the inherent unity of the gospel narratives must be considered the most salient single feature of narrative criticism.

At this very central point, however, serious confusion begins to appear. The seeds of this confusion lie in the fact that many narrative critics, so it seems, use one and the same term, 'narrative unity,' in two different

---

[16] Thus also Moore 1989, 51–55; Moore 1994, 67–68, 131.
[17] Rhoads 1994, 343; cf. Rhoads and Michie 1982, 3.

senses. First, they maintain that a narrative analysis of the gospels *shows* the gospels to be 'of remarkably whole cloth.'[18] This *argument of unity* implies that unity is a *discovery*, or a result of analysis. Second, narrative criticism makes an *assumption of unity*, that is to say, it opts for a holistic approach that *a priori* sees every narrative as an autonomous, inherently unified world. In light of this,

> Narrative unity is not something that must be proved from an analysis of the material. Rather, it is something that can be assumed. It is the form of narrative itself that grants coherence to the material, no matter how disparate that material might be . . . The presence of inconsistencies in no way undermines the unity of a narrative but simply becomes one of the facets to be interpreted. They may, for instance, signal gaps and ambiguities that must be either explained or held in tension. This is true regardless of whether they are there by design or negligence . . . the real question is whether the poetic function of the gospels in the form that we now have them is a worthwhile subject for investigation.[19]

Let us first acknowledge the point here. The assumption of unity – that is, the licence to seek meaning or reason for any aspect of the story first inside the story itself – opens up new possibilities to argue for interpretations that reveal previously unrecognized patterns of unity in the text.[20] This is certainly true. Now, the salient point is that the two ways of understanding narrative unity must not be confused.[21] Otherwise, we end up moving in circles. If narrative critics wish to argue for a *particular* unity and coherence of the gospel narratives (which they do, whenever they say that 'analyses of the formal features of the gospel of Mark have shown this narrative to be of remarkably whole cloth'), they will have to *prove* their case, *from an analysis of the material*, to their fellow scholars, whether in the biblical or in the literary field.

In both cases, resistance should be expected. On the one hand, the more traditionally-oriented biblical critics are likely to continue their complaints that narrative critics ignore or too easily dismiss inconsistencies in the gospels due to the differences between traditions and redactions in the gospel material. On the other hand, the perils of seeing

---

[18] Rhoads 1994, 343; cf. Rhoads and Michie 1982, 3.
[19] Powell 1990, 92, 93.
[20] Cf. Tolbert 1989, 31.
[21] Actually, there are two key questions involved here. The other is whether (or which of) those patterns are really *in the text*. I will return to this in due course.

too much unity and coherence in narratives are widely recognized in contemporary literary scholarship as well. Let us consider this issue first from a historical-critical, then from a literary-theoretical point of view.

Put simply, historical-critical scholars of the Bible fear that narrative-critical analyses smooth over inconsistencies and breaks in the text in favor of harmonizing interpretations. Such practice would be made possible by the narrative-critical 'assumption of unity' that, from the point of the more traditional biblical criticism, is equal to the practice of 'verdict first, trial second.' If *any feature* of *any text* can be interpreted in terms of the unity of the whole, there should, indeed, be no point in concluding that *some particular text* is 'remarkably unified.'

Apparently, however, a number of narrative critics feel tempted to have it both ways. Consider Jeffrey Lloyd Staley's analysis of *the implied reader* of the Fourth Gospel.[22] As Staley puts it, a holistic, text-centered approach allows the critic to assume that every detail of the text plays a significant part in the narrator's rhetorical strategy. John's narrative strategy is, according to Staley, based on what Staley calls 'the victimization of the reader.'[23] Once critics recognize this strategy, it will help them to analyze contradictory passages in the gospel in terms of their effect upon the reader rather than in terms of their compositional history.[24] The critic may regard all the 'narrative-busting elements as heavily ironized rhetorical ploys' that 'force the implied reader into the role of an outsider, an error-prone reader who can never feel as though his grasp of Jesus or the life of faith is absolute.'[25]

Most passages in John that, in Staley's view, 'victimize' the reader are passages that traditional scholarship has sought to explain by referring to the multilayered editing of the gospel. In the beginning of John 4,

---

[22] Staley 1988; cf. also Staley 1993. Staley himself places these studies in the context of *reader-response criticism* (Staley 1988, 6). Nevertheless, his primary methodological starting-point is a narratological one, namely Seymour Chatman's model of narrative communication (Staley 1988, 21ff.). Because Staley's main focus is on how the narrator, as inscribed *in the text*, controls the reading process, his method does not differ essentially from narrative criticism.

[23] Staley borrows the term 'reader victimization' from McKee 1974; see Staley 1988, 95, n. 1; Staley 1993, 83 n. 21. Staley admits that the term is usually used in connection with modern novels. Nevertheless, as he notes, the term is not anachronistic in the Hellenistic era. A narrator who makes use of the strategy of reader victimization resembles the Socratic εἴϱων who also 'feigns ignorance and occasionally suppresses his own knowledge in order to educate his audience' (Staley 1993, 84).

[24] Staley 1988, 96.

[25] Staley 1993, 82–83.

for example, there is a narrative comment which most critics would take as a later editorial gloss. In the course of the narrative, the narrator notes twice that Jesus baptized (3:22; 4:1). The comment in 4:1 is followed by an awkward correction that says that it was not Jesus himself but his disciples who baptized (4:2). It is customary to regard this correction as a secondary attempt to establish a clear difference between Jesus and John the Baptist. As such, the verse 'serves as almost indisputable evidence of the presence of several hands in the composition of John.'[26] Staley, however, claims that the comment has a rhetorical function. It forces the implied reader to 're-evaluate his relationship to the narrator and the story;' the implied reader 'finds that he had only been set up to be hoodwinked by the juxtaposition of 3:22 and 4:2.' The narrator seeks 'to force the implied reader to realize that in spite of his high degree of knowledge, he still does not know everything. The gospel, as well as being an aesthetic whole, is a "learning program."'[27] Other passages that, according to Staley, make the Fourth Gospel a 'learning program' contain similar dissonance that traditional scholarship would explain by referring to different redactional layers. In Staley's eyes, all these passages have a rhetorical purpose.[28]

Certainly, such a literary-rhetorical reading of John as Staley's is possible. Yet one may ask – and a historical critic will be likely to ask – whether that kind of reading comes naturally. After all, before Staley, not one real reader of the gospel has ever grasped the 'rhetorical ploys' that supposedly hide in its seemingly contradictory passages. Instead,

---

[26] Brown 1966, 164.

[27] Staley 1988, 98.

[28] In addition to John 4:1–2, these passages include 7:1–10, where Jesus says he is not going to the festival (v. 8), whereas the narrator says that Jesus did go to the festival (v. 10); 10:40–11:18, where the narrator's information concerning the location of Bethany is confusing as compared to earlier information according to which Bethany was beyond Jordan (1:28); 13:1–30, where the unexpected appearance of an unnamed character called 'the beloved disciple' takes the reader by surprise; 20:35–21:25, where the reader is 'victimized' by the unexpected prolonging of the story at the beginning of chap. 21, and by the enigmatic closure of the narrative (21:24–25). These passages mark a process of growth which the implied reader goes through: at first, the implied reader is an outsider in company with the antagonistic Pharisees (chap. 4); then, the narrator moves the implied reader into the company of Jesus' unbelieving brothers (chap. 7); next, the implied reader is a few steps behind the disciples who misunderstand Jesus (chap. 11); then, the implied reader is at the same level with the surprised disciples (chap. 13); finally, the implied reader shares Peter's position (chap. 21). (See Staley 1988, 116.) Later, Staley included John 18:12–24 among the Johannine passages that 'victimize the reader.' (See Staley 1993.)

these passages have provoked one real reader after another to produce either overtly harmonizing interpretations or critical hypotheses about the composition history of the gospel. Thus, in Staley's view, the whole history of John's interpretation is full of readers who have become victims of the Johannine narrator's rhetoric.[29] Is there not, however, something utterly disturbing in the idea that the Johannine narrator's rhetoric, supposedly comparable even to the irony of the Socratic dialogue, is only revealed to one modern and sensitive critic, and that the text's entire earlier reception history consists of misunderstandings, misreadings and misinterpretations? Why is there so little evidence that any real readers ever experienced the text in the way Staley describes?[30]

Historical scholarship, for its part, might claim double evidence for its case. First, historical critics can refer to the comparative study of Early Jewish and Early Christian literature to explain why there is genuine dissonance in the text. In the light of comparative study, we know that these writings often went through an editing process; one evangelist used the text of another as a source; comments, corrections and additions found their way into the text. Second, historical scholarship may look at how some early historical readers responded to the text; this helps to clarify what type of readings the text seems to invite, as well as to assess how successful some rhetorical strategy, supposedly contained in the text, might have been in actual rhetorical situations. Thus it seems that, supported by no historical conventions of reading, a reading such as Staley's is a forced one. Indeed, we have to ask whether Staley is not simply trying, by means of literary analysis, to *prove* that John can be read as a unity, which, in turn, would make John a legitimate object of literary analysis.

---

[29] For example, in John 18:24–24, there is a text-critical problem that Staley regards as an example of 'reader victimization:' having first mentioned that Jesus was questioned by the high priest (18:19–23), the text states that Jesus was sent to Caiaphas the high priest (v. 24). Several different manuscripts have addressed this problem by reordering the text. According to Staley, it is these attempts as well as 'numerous commentators' notes that paradoxically testify to the narrative's rhetorical power at the very moment those same real readers are falling victim to it.' See Staley 1993, 96–97.

[30] Cf. Moore 1989, 106, on applications of reader-response criticism to the gospels: 'Hearing how the implied reader of the gospels forms expectations here only to revise them there . . ., I am compelled to ask: Why do I experience none of these things when I read the text? Why is there so little evidence that the Church, historically, experienced them? And does the reader-critic who pulls the readers strings actually experience them either?'

Notably, the historical critics of the Bible are not the only ones to resist harmonizing readings. Narratologists, for example, had no specific interest in showing or assuming that narratives, some of them or all of them, are inherently unified. It was meant to be a descriptive theory, not a method of criticism. The models it proposed were designed to give a comprehensive formal description of any given narrative, no matter how unified or disjointed that narrative might be. In the closing lines of his *Narrative Discourse: An Essay in Method,* a distinguished classic of narrative theory, Gérard Genette, explicitly refuses to end his description of the narrative structures present in Marcel Proust's *À la recherche du temps perdu* with a final synthesis that would show the inherent unity and coherence of Proustian narrative. This is because such unity and coherence is not to be found, and it would be 'unfortunate . . . to seek "unity" at any price, and in that way to *force* the work's coherence – which is, of course, one of criticism's strongest temptations, one of its most ordinary (not to say most common) ones, and also most easy to satisfy, since all it requires is a little interpretative rhetoric.'[31]

Reading for unity is second nature in criticism. In another highly influential work of literary theory, *The Genesis of Secrecy: On the Interpretation of Narrative* (1979), Frank Kermode uses the very New Testament interpretation as a case in point to show how successive interpreters always seek and find more and more unity and coherence in the text. Aptly, Kermode calls all critics of all canons 'pleromatists,' 'fulfilment men,' 'programmed to prefer fulfilment to disappointment, the closed to the open.'[32] For a professional critic, this fulfilment is never hard to find; 'techniques of literary criticism provide us with a range of devices for eliciting unified interpretations from apparent inconsequentiality; we are familiar with concepts of ambiguity, irony, symbolism, and other kinds of literary indirectness that help us bring *prima facie* ill-formed texts under proper control.'[33] Staley's reading of the gospel of John is a perfect example of this.

While a narratologist like Genette may, for the sake of keeping descriptive poetics accurate, warn against forcing the literary work's coherence, poststructuralist critics of narratology go further and deny

---

[31] Genette 1980 (1972), 266. On the independence of narrative criticism from narratology, see Moore 1989, 51–55.

[32] Kermode 1979, 64, 72.

[33] Heath 1989, 1–2.

narratological models their internal coherence. As these critics maintain, theoretical models are not universal structures but rather represent contingent constructions that are, as such, deconstructable.

Where applied as a critical method, literary deconstruction specializes in readings that demonstrate how texts successfully resist critics' attempts to perceive them as coherent, integral wholes. In gospel studies, Stephen D. Moore has done pioneering work in this field.[34] In his treatment of water symbolism in the gospel of John, Moore seeks to show that John's narrative does not allow such a fixed, stable way of interpreting the concept 'water' as would be necessary for a fully coherent reading of the gospel as a whole. At Jacob's well, the reader needs to take the words 'water' and 'thirst' in a spiritual sense in order to grasp the Johannine irony. However, when Jesus later asks for and receives a drink on the cross, and when fresh water flows from his side, it is essential that both 'thirst' and 'water' are material; this is a necessary precondition for the symbolic level of the narrative to work at all. So the narrative suddenly changes its basic rules of making sense – with the result that its internal logic collapses.[35] While Moore's analysis might be considered a rather tendentious counter-reading of narrative-critical approaches to John and the other gospels, it nevertheless drives home the point that, in the end, no descriptive model is truly descriptive. Models do not replicate any objective structures present in the text as such. Rather, they each produce another text, another narrative whose structures mirror the interests of those who developed the model and those who apply it.

Unity as Standard

The assumption of unity that marks the work of many narrative critics is thus a tricky issue. Once we allow ourselves to seek meaning for any aspect of the story first in the story itself, the thin line between analysis and interpretation begins to grow obscure.[36] In so far as interpretation

---

[34] See Moore 1992; Moore 1994. Other applications of deconstruction to biblical studies include e.g. Jobling 1990; Jobling 1992; Burnett 1991; Seeley 1994; Bubar 1995.

[35] See e.g. Moore 1994, chap. 2, 'Deconstructive Criticism: Derrida at the Samaritan Well and, Later, at the Foot of the Cross,' pp. 43–64. The same textual example appears in many of Moore's writings.

[36] Some theorists would simply say that no such line exists; remember Bloom's slogan, '*There are no texts, only readings.*'

is what we do, there is, basically, no limit to the meaningful connections we can make in a given text. However disparate the material, it can be interpreted as a unity. Therefore, the assumption of unity will not, as such, make an argument for unity.[37]

Another problem relates to the fact that the unity achieved by means of interpretation is taken – explicitly or implicitly – as a (or even the) criterion of literary value. In practice, the validity of this criterion is considered more or less a given. This is done by narrative critics and historical critics alike. Both of them would expect the gospels to be 'remarkably unified,' if they were to appreciate them as good literature. Correspondingly, they assume that inconsequentiality in the gospels, should there be any, must be seen as a deficiency – a case of bad design or a sign of the text's corruption. While historical critics refer to points of incoherence and use these points to argue that the gospels fail to satisfy as literary works, narrative critics assume that inconsequentiality is merely apparent, and go on to propose integrated interpretations that establish overarching themes or structures that hold the seemingly incoherent elements together.

On the other hand, while the criterion of unity is hardly a universal given, it certainly is part of an ancient and well-established tradition. In his *Poetics*, Aristotle says that the parts of a tragedy 'must be so arranged that if one of them be transposed or removed, the unity of the whole is dislocated and destroyed. For if the presence or absence of a thing makes no visible difference, then it is not an integral part of the whole' (*Poetics* 1451a, trans. W. H. Fyfe). Likewise, according to Horace's classic formulation, the literary work should be *simplex et unum* (*Ars Poetica*, 23).

Thus, even at the time when the gospels were written, the standard was there – which may lead us to ponder the question whether the evangelists themselves might have hoped that their works would turn out to be successes by this standard. After all, each evangelist bothered to compose a linear, sequentially ordered narrative. Luke, for one, set out 'to write *an orderly account*' (καθεξῆς γράψαι) of what was 'handed

---

[37] It is also contestable, we might add, that *any* epistemologically valid arguments for or against the unity – or any other inherent feature – of texts are available at all. If Stanley Fish is right, it is positively impossible to bypass interpretation and just analyze the 'text itself.' This is because *interpretation is what constitutes 'a text.'* Without interpretation there would be only ink stains on white paper. (This is the argument developed progressively in Fish's 1980 collection *Is There a Text in This Class?*)

on to us' (Luke 1:2, 3), and let his audience know that other people, too, had undertaken a similar task (Luke 1:1).

At the same time, it is evident that the evangelists had this type of ambition only up to a certain point. Certainly, they introduced redactional additions, stylistic corrections, and some re-organizing to the material that they used as their source – in the manner we (who use the *two-source hypothesis*) may witness Matthew and Luke to have treated their sources (that is, Mark and the sayings source *Q*). Yet it is equally apparent that they did not consistently throw away or completely rewrite elements that failed to serve the whole. Taken as a whole, the performance of the evangelists seems rather to testify that they were not only, or even primarily, conducting an aesthetic enterprise. Instead, they worked to promote what they understood to be an ideologically viable interpretation of an essentially historical message that was to be preserved in an authentic form.

At this point, we must also ask how much unity and coherence the literary standards of the ancient Greek poetics would actually have required. In a wider perspective, there seems to be – to quote Malcolm Heath – a 'relative lack of interest in the concept of unity in ancient criticism; where it does play an important role – notably in Aristotle's *Poetics* . . . the criteria of unity applied [are] tolerant of [diverging,] centrifugal practices.'[38] Besides, the very notion of unity itself appears to be subject to historical and cultural change: it seems that when the ancient Greek critics spoke of unity, they did not think so much of thematic integrity and interrelatedness.[39] Rather, they understood the unity of the work to mean that everything in its design on the formal level served the ends of the genre to which it belonged.[40] Plato thought that the philosopher should be free to ignore the requirements of formal composition as long as his or her arguments succeeded in attaining the truth.[41] This is exactly the same point that Bishop Papias of Hierapolis made in the second century CE in order to defend the

---

[38] Heath 1989, 9. At this point, Heath is referring to an earlier discussion in Heath 1987.

[39] Heath 1989, 3.

[40] Heath 1989, 150. In Aristotle's case, we must indeed note that 'his concern is limited to unity in "mimetic" genres, such as epic and drama, and he explicitly contrasts the criteria applicable to those genres with the standards appropriate to historiography' (Heath 1989, 38). Also, 'he is not concerned, as Plato was, with the organization of the literary text as such, but with the underlying structure of its plot' (Heath 1989, 151).

[41] See *Theaetetus* 172de; Heath 1989, 22, 26.

apparently disintegrated structure of Mark's gospel. According to Papias, the gospel's lack of order is not important, because the evangelist nevertheless succeeds in telling the truth about the apostle Peter's preaching.[42]

Thus, on a very basic level, the gospels might perhaps be considered unified enough to meet the goal-oriented and genre-specific standards of their time. Their primary goal was not beauty but truth; they were written 'so that you may come to believe' (John 20:31) or 'so that you may know the truth as it was handed on to us' (cf. Luke 1:2). In the end, this self-appointed *telos* – especially the need to be faithful to traditions used as sources – necessarily meant accepting a considerable amount of diversity in literary presentation. This was sometimes considered a problem (as Luke's opening and Papias' comment on Mark seem to indicate), but still a relatively minor one. Ultimately, the treasure inside was considered far more precious than the clay jars that contained it (cf. 2 Cor. 4:7).[43]

Later, of course, the clay jars were put neatly into a golden casket. Although the early patristic apology that one should not expect divine truth to veil itself in human standards of eloquence has been repeated several times in subsequent history, the Bible came to establish a position in the center of the Western cultural canon and became a prominent intertext to an entire legion of discourses whose high cultural status was not a matter for questioning.[44] Once this had taken place, the gospels did not really have to show outward signs of unity in order to remain texts of literary significance. If ever unity – or some other criterion of literary value – became that strictly required, it would be rather easy to constitute a sufficient amount of it by means of literary interpretation. After all, as pointed out by Kermode, Heath and others, that is what interpretation is for.

By virtue of interpretation, everyone who searches may find the values he or she is looking for. As contexts and their prevalent values change,

---

[42] Eusebius, *Hist. eccl.* 3.35.15 (Eusebius quotes from Papias' lost work, *Expositions of the Words of the Lord*, which apparently dates from *c.*140 CE). On the other hand, one must note that Papias felt it necessary to defend Mark's work.

[43] This is not to say that the treasure inside is a single and unified one. For conflicting ideological elements in Paul's thinking, see Räisänen 1987, esp. pp. 199–202; in Matthew, Syreeni 1990, 3–13.

[44] For a comprehensive account of how people have thought of the Bible and Bible translations (especially the King James Version) from biblical times to the present day, see Norton 1993a and Norton 1993b.

readings will change with them. If canonical texts are to remain canonical, they will have to be Jewish to the Jews and Greek to the Greeks. So, if the current vogue of postmodernism has brought with it 'a suspicion of totalities' and raised fragmentariness as its core value,[45] those reading the gospels for signs of literary significance will be likely to focus on entirely different matters than unity and coherence. Before long, the most intriguing literary aspects of the gospels may again seem to relate to the aspects of *diversity and dissonance* which these narratives display.

In *Problems of Dostoevsky's Poetics* (1929, Engl. trans. 1984) – a work of immense inspiration for postmodernist literary criticism – Mikhail Bakhtin hailed the Russian literary genius Fyodor Dostoevsky as the inventor of an entirely new form of literary expression, namely the *polyphonic novel*. According to Bakhtin, polyphonic narration is characterized by the principle of *dialogism*, that is, interaction among several voices, consciousnesses, and world views, none of which is allowed to rule over the others.

At first sight, as ideological literature whose omniscient narrators constantly seek to control their characters and readers, the gospels may not seem likely to qualify as dialogic narratives in the full Bakhtinian sense of the word. Rather, they present a paradigm case of what Bakhtin called *monologic*, or *authoritative* discourse.

On the other hand, however, it is exactly the multivoicedness of the biblical text that decades of historical biblical criticism have brought to daylight. On the surface level, innumerable scholarly readings have discovered features of several different (oral and literary) genres and discursive practices. Under the surface, a multitude of different traditions is encountered, each claiming its share of truth out of a different historical, social and ideological context.[46] It is not difficult to see that, in contemporary literary avant-garde culture with its resistance to stability, closure and dominance, this dissonant, unsettled appearance of the gospels might find a perfect match.[47]

*

[45] Kermode 1988, 133.
[46] These aspects have recently been emphasized by W. L. Reed (1993), and M. Jones (1996).
[47] Cf. also Moore 1994, 66–74.

Unity in the gospels is easily achieved through literary interpretation, but so are diversity and fragmentariness. In fact, we may even ask whether it is possible to have one without the other. Every construction of unity is deconstructable, and the very concept of fragment seems to imply a totality that has become lost. In some peculiar sense, to hold both aspects simultaneously seems 'both fatal and necessary.'[48]

What is certain is that, as literary values, both unity and fragmentariness must be seen as particular and historical, not as universal or timeless. The same goes, as a consequence, for any concept of canon and literature. As no objective criteria of good literature can be successfully demonstrated, how '*Volksliteratur*' or '*Kleinliteratur*' can be distinguished from 'literature proper' will depend on personal or institutional choice as conditioned by historical and ideological circumstances. This means that, at least to some assemblies, the gospels may, for once, come as they are.

---

[48] Kermode 1988, 141, with reference to Friedrich Schlegel.

3

Why do Modern Readers value Mark?

Having established that conceptions of literary meaning and value are historically contingent I would like to linger on this issue for a while, so as to fully explore its consequences for practical analysis.

For the composer, and for every new audience, literary composition first becomes meaningful and valuable in a particular historical and cultural situation. Even if we choose to bracket the real historical composer and audiences and focus exclusively on strategies of storytelling and reading as presupposed by or encoded in the text (narratologists would call these the *implied* or *model author* and *reader*, respectively), the situation will not be radically altered – because these strategies, too, change, when we move from one time or culture to another. This suggests that we reckon with the historical and cultural moments of production and reception in the analysis.

This is to say that formal analysis of texts should be hermeneutical.[1] It needs to have regard for the conditions that regulate the dialogue between two historical parties, the (critical) reader and the text. For this reason, it will be concerned with the reception and valuation of historical works as an objectifiable, yet perpetually ongoing and open-ended process which situates in and constitutes a particular historical moment comparable to the analyst's own.[2]

As a case in point, in this chapter I will briefly assess the recent reception and (re)valuation of a familiar New Testament narrative in a

---

[1] What I just presented in a sweeping summary indeed connects to a prominent trajectory in the history of philosophical hermeneutics. This trajectory originates in Wilhelm Dilthey's insight that, as an object of understanding in humanistic studies, human culture is profoundly historical, and leads to the hermeneutic philosophies of Martin Heidegger and Hans-Georg Gadamer that properly emphasize the inescapable historicity of the *understanding subject*.

[2] This is also assumed as the starting point in Hans Robert Jauss' *Rezeptionsästhetik* – a synthesis influenced by (among other things) Russian Formalist and Czech structuralist poetics as well as Gadamer's hermeneutics. See Jauss 1982.

historical moment and geographical setting that is conveniently close to my own. That is, I will consider what has happened lately to Mark's gospel in my cultural neighborhood. It seems to me that many recent literary readings of Mark adhere to a traditional dichotomy between the aesthetic (or the literary) and the ideological. The literary qualities of the gospel are seen to exist *in spite of* or *in dissonance with* its ideological aims. In other words, these qualities are considered either unintentional by-products of ideological writing or a fatal error in rhetorical strategy, finally deconstructing every attempt to proclaim some unequivocal ideological message (indeed, *gospel*). This will lead to the crucial question: what is, accurately described, the relationship between poetics and ideology in the gospels?

Mark's Long Way to the Top

In 1996 the author of Mark's gospel (identified as John Mark) received a notable collegial tribute when the award-winning Finnish poet Gösta Ågren published a collection, *The Carpenter*, based on the gospel. In the introduction to his work, Ågren praises (John) Mark as a cunning author: 'Solid, concrete structure gives strength to the story. The author is frank and lucid. Legendary material is not allowed to dominate, yet it flavors the events.'[3] On another occasion – in a newspaper interview – Ågren put the matter even more frankly and praised Mark as 'the best-written among the gospels – *the most literary*' (my emphasis).

Ågren's acclaim of Mark is matched in biblical studies by the recent positive assessment of this gospel by narrative critics. Moreover, Mark the great artist has been enthusiastically rediscovered by the general public: theater performances of the gospel have played to full houses in Norway, Sweden and Finland.

Historically, Mark's literary breakthrough came very late. For hundreds of years, the first narrative gospel was considered the last among the gospels. In the earliest surviving account of Mark's reception, Papias felt it necessary to excuse the gospel's apparent lack of order.[4] Some two hundred years later, Augustine expressed the opinion that Mark was merely an abbreviated version of Matthew.[5] This view

[3] Ågren 1996, 6 (my translation).
[4] Cf. above, pp. 31–32.
[5] Augustine, *On the Agreement of the Evangelists*, 1.2.4.

remained dominant all through the Middle Ages, ensuring that Mark would stay in the shadow of the three other, assumedly more valuable gospels: Matthew, the first and foremost gospel in the Western church; Luke, whose memorable, educational novellas would give him a reputation as an early Christian 'master of the short story;'[6] John, 'the spiritual gospel' that withheld from popular storytelling and simple moral paradigms to reveal the one and only divine truth the reader will ever need to know.

Mark's demise continued in modern critical scholarship. While scholars eventually became convinced that Mark was the earliest of the New Testament gospels – which, of course, made his work very interesting historically – they still held the gospel in low esteem in literary terms. As I noted before, the gospels in general were not regarded as literature in the strict sense of the word. Scholars rather considered them popular ideological writings, strings of pearls of traditional material, whose proper setting was not the literary institution, but early Christian cult and proclamation.

Mark in particular was considered to have failed as an author. Classics of biblical criticism agreed with Papias on Mark's lack of proper order: 'Mark is not sufficiently master of his material to be able to venture on a systematic construction himself.'[7] In full contrast to Ågren's judgment, not only did critics accuse the gospel of being disintegrated and lacking in order, they also emphasized the prominent role that the miracle stories – Ågren's 'properly subordinate' 'legendary material' – play in the composition of the whole.[8]

And then, suddenly, Mark was discovered – by authors, narrative critics and the public.

What happened? Why did it take so long for him to find a receptive literary audience – and what made this audience so well-suited for this purpose? What makes Mark's story such that it fits the modern reader's ideals and expectations?[9]

Technically, what happened was *revaluation*: an old text, apparently neglected through ignorance, was 'made new by association or

---

[6] Drury 1987, 427.
[7] Bultmann 1968 (1931), 350. 'A systematic *outline*' would probably be a more accurate translation of the original German word, '*Gliederung.*'
[8] See e.g. Theissen 1983 (1974), 212 n. 25.
[9] Some empirically supported answers to these questions will be provided in Marja Vuohiniemi's forthcoming study based on interviews with members of the audience of Mark's Gospel in Tampere City Theatre in 1999.

application.'[10] Actually, in the history of literary reception, a similar phenomenon appears to have taken place often enough to become something like standard practice. This time, in Mark's case, the narrative's assumed modernity has come to be viewed in the light of two dominant aesthetic traditions of modern times, that is, the tradition of realism and the tradition of modernism.[11]

Mark's Realism

In his 1946 modern classic *Mimesis: The Representation of Reality in Western Literature*, Erich Auerbach suggests that the narrative art of the early Christian gospels transcends the limits of the ancient, classical representation of reality in a way that corresponds to modern realism's takeoff from classicism at the beginning of the 19th century. As an example, he discusses the story of Peter's denial according to the gospel of Mark. As Auerbach notes, this story is a noble as well as a tragic one, unique in its significance as a dramatic part of the divine plan for the salvation of humankind, yet at the same time commonly recognizable. Struggling with himself on the stage of holy history, Peter is the image of humanity 'in the highest and deepest and most tragic sense.'[12]

What makes the scene of Peter's denial different from classic literary ideals – and what brings it close to modern literary realism – is the fact that it combines the tragic and the universal with the common and the ordinary. A story which claims to have universal – indeed, cosmic – significance yet focuses on everyday reality, that is, on the personal failure of an average individual of low social rank, as witnessed by a group of servants. In his perfect commonality, Peter could really be anyone. Compared to any destined-to-be-hero of a classical work, the appointment of this Galilean fisherman to his dramatic role gives a peculiar impression of randomness.

---

[10] Kermode 1988, 124.

[11] Since the chapter was written, Nick Cave's assessment of Mark's gospel has appeared in *Harper's Magazine*. Emphasizing Mark's impassioned intensity and expressive power, Cave's essay fittingly represents the third great tradition of modern Western aesthetics, namely *expressionism*. As a third piece of evidence, then, this looks very much like a final confirmation of Frank Kermode's claim that 'isms' 'inevitably involve evaluation' (Kermode 1988, 121).

[12] Auerbach 1953 (1946), 41.

According to the requirements of classical style, the representation of common, everyday reality properly belongs to comedy.[13] A modern audience, in turn, would be accustomed to regarding this kind of realism as a central precondition of any effectively authentic tragedy: in order to evoke 'fear and pity,' the action depicted needs to be such that it might actually happen to *real* (that is, *ordinary*) people in *real* (that is, *common*) life.

In this respect, Mark would indeed need little adaptation in order to work on the modern stage or screen. The gospel's mimetic standards accord with modern preferences. Rapid cuts keep the camera in constant motion. Characters like servant-girls and fishermen – ordinary people 'just like us' – engage in brief, direct dialogues in a common language. The protagonist of the story is a witty yet somewhat antisocial popular hero who is regularly at odds with the authorities . . . At the same time, of course, the protagonist is also the Son of the Most High God, in a story that comprises most classic ingredients. The overall plot rests upon great peripeteia and recognition: the triumphant redeemer ends up on the cross, the extreme Power hides in its ultimate opposite. In the end, the strong impact the story makes is due to the breakdown of difference between the levels of high and low style. The tragic and the noble mix with the crude and the common. According to Auerbach, this very mixture is also the salient characteristic of modern literary realism.[14]

Naturally, the gospels are not meant to be realistic, at least not in the literary-stylistic sense of the word. Auerbach, too, emphasizes the apparent accidentality of the gospels' literary merits.[15] In this respect, he agrees with traditional biblical scholarship: the gospels lack high literary ambition as well as – by the standards of their time – genuine literary skill. In literary terms, they are in an age of innocence; infant geniuses as they were, they transform artistic expression unawares, with no intention of so doing.

What, then, brought about this beneficial mixing of styles, if not the author's creative will? According to Auerbach, the literary realism among the early Christians, as well as in the early 19th century, was a result of a particular historical and ideological need: suddenly, it became necessary to depict a world, not a stable and unchanging state of order, but invaded

---

[13] Auerbach 1953 (1946), 44.
[14] Auerbach 1953 (1946), 40, 554–555.
[15] Auerbach 1953 (1946), 47.

by fundamental transformations that concerned everybody – or *anyone*. This reality could not be grasped by following classicist rules of style. This was because those rules made sense of the world by adjusting human experiences of it to fixed categories, moral and rhetorical. As to portraying a historical movement that took shape and became concrete – in unforeseeable ways – in common everyday life, those categories had not much to offer.[16]

Mark's Modernism

If Auerbach is right, the gospels are avant-garde created by chance – noble savages happily saved from the restraining influences of their contemporary high culture and its stiff literary establishment. In the narratives, weakness becomes strength in a way that Papias was clever enough to note in Mark's defense: the absence of conventional rhetoric, style and order bears witness not only to the work's primitive nature, but also to the authenticity of the story it has to tell. In this respect, it is indeed Mark that, no doubt, is the most savage and the most noble of all.[17]

In Mark, the ideals of authenticity, originality and naturalness involve yet another level that also has marked points of contact with modern literary values. Besides being stylistically the most primitive, and thus, implicitly, the most original gospel, Mark is also the one which displays the greatest amount of ambiguity – and thus, implicitly, the most virginal experience of meaning.[18] As many scholars have aptly remarked, this

---

[16] Auerbach 1953 (1946), 40, 43–45.

[17] Originally, the idea of a 'distinction between mortal eloquence and divine truth' appeared as early as in Paul: 'My speech and my proclamation were not with plausible words of wisdom, but with the demonstration of the Spirit and of power, so that your faith might rest not on human wisdom but on the power of God' (1 Cor. 2:4–5). Later, this 'anti-aesthetic' that views the lack of aesthetic quality in the form as having a positive value is programmatically entertained by such early church fathers as Justin Martyr, Tatian and Tertullian (and, later, John Chrysostom – as well as many others); for all of them, the lack of classic rhetoric is in itself an argument for the truthfulness of the biblical text. (See Norton 1993a, 14–23.)

[18] Like his realism, Mark's ambiguity is hardly fully intentional. Like the other gospels, Mark, too, is ideological literature with a clear interest in univocal meaning. Sometimes ambiguity may be used for rhetorical purposes, yet the ideological aims of the narrative set a limit to making the message seem obscure. (See further chap. 5 below.) However, especially in cases in which he is trying to *address two situations at the same time* – namely the situation of the historical characters in the story, and the current situation of his

gospel reminds us of a *parable* of which the final, conclusive meaning remains difficult for anyone to catch.[19] Whereas Matthew and Luke present their stories much more directly as sources of value and codes of conduct, in Mark we must repeatedly *seek* after meaning. In Mark's story, Jesus' kingship is a secret, his parabolic words and deeds, as well as his fate, are signs that need to be interpreted correctly.[20] Yet *the discovery of meaning*, the solution of the riddles, the transformation of parabolic teaching into paradigms, models of action, rules of moral conduct, a way to salvation – any one of these features only rarely, if at all.

Those who should understand – those to whom 'has been given the secret of the kingdom of God' (Mark 4:10), the disciples – will not. Experiencing miracles will not cause them to have faith or gain insight. They find it utterly difficult to follow Jesus' teaching and imitate his example. For them, the necessity of Jesus' passion and the reality of the resurrection are simply incomprehensible. When Jesus' hour has come, they abandon their Master and flee.[21]

By implication, Mark's general inconclusiveness culminates in the dramatic anticlimax at the narrative's ending, an ending which is a grammatical rarity in itself. The reader's expectations of a final moment of recognition, a long-awaited opening of the eyes, are met only with an enduring blindness, fear and silence. In Jesus' tomb, a small group of women learn that he has indeed risen from the dead. They are told to bring the good news to the disciples. Then the narrative abruptly ends with these words: 'So they went out and fled from the tomb, for terror and amazement had seized them; and they said nothing to anyone, for they were afraid' (Mark 16:8).

The last word of the story is a feeble particle γάρ. For a long time, scholars believed that it was not possible to end even a sentence with such a structure. Now we know that this was, indeed, possible in popular

---

intended audience – Mark does not always seem to master his material sufficiently. What results are mixed messages, inconsistent narrative patterns, unintenional ambiguity. (Thus Räisänen 1990; see esp. pp. 19–21.)

[19] Donahue 1978; Kelber 1983.

[20] For a comprehensive analysis of the secrecy theme in Mark, see Räisänen 1990.

[21] Like the secrecy theme, the role of the disciples in Mark is a classic topic. For a concise introduction to scholarly discussion, see Matera 1987, 38–55. For an analysis, see Räisänen 1990, 195–221.

Greek. Yet there is no other known case of an entire narrative ending that way.

This ending proved to be impossible for many early readers of Mark to accept. Several early Christian scribes who made new manuscript copies of the gospel ended up continuing it. Consequently, several secondary, longer endings exist in manuscript traditions. They all serve the purpose of giving an ending – a definite happy ending – to a story that appeared to lack one.

A story that ended like Mark might even make a modern reader confused – unless that reader were aware that he or she was reading a modern literary work of art whose known salient characteristics included the inconvenient absence of a satisfactory ending. With insight, Frank Kermode compares Mark's final word γάρ to the closing words of *Ulysses* and *Finnegans Wake* by James Joyce, those words being the English words 'yes' and 'the,' respectively.[22]

The openness, undecidability, and ambivalence in Mark also serve as literary gateways from the ancient to the modern in *The Carpenter* by Ågren. These features of the Markan narrative direct the reader to see that meaning resides not in the interpretation of the narrative, but in the narrative form itself. As Ågren puts it, in his poem 'Parables,' 'If the interpretation of the parable said it all, one would need no parable.'

The absence of any closed, final meaning plays a central role in Ågren's own interpretation of Mark. He articulates this idea first in the opening poem of *The Carpenter*, 'Expedition:' 'There was no end; otherwise, the journey itself would have made no sense.' Later, he returns to the same idea in the collection's concluding poem, 'Daybreak:' 'The longing for news is the only news that makes it through.'

Mark's gospel becomes lyric poetry in Ågren's reading. As such, it is purged into a perfect language of images; no articulate, readable message will stain its eternally virginal desire for meaning.

Mark's Claim of Originality

For a modern reader, Mark's innate realism and ambiguity are artistic values that relate to an impression of authenticity and originality mediated by the work's literary form. On the other hand, for most of its existence, the gospel's worth (or worthlessness) has been associated

---

[22] Kermode 1979, 66–67.

with a very similar ideal as regards to its subject matter. Papias made a connection between Mark and Peter, and sought to assure people that the gospel reiterated the apostle's original voice as faithfully as possible. Augustine denied Mark value by claiming that the gospel was an inauthentic secondary version of Matthew. Modern scholarship laid the basis for Mark's rehabilitation by confirming its status as the earliest and, consequently, the most original gospel.

A certain impression of originality must, in all probability, also have been among the aims of the evangelist himself. Notably, in his case this concerned both the message and the medium, as interrelated. He wished to ensure that his truth about Jesus, of all the truths available, was to be accepted as normative. For this purpose, he composed a narrative that reveals – realistically, as it were – the true origin of the good news of Jesus Christ (cf. Mark 1:1). Later, other evangelists would do the same, each of them trying to get as close to the beginning as possible. Thus, Matthew opens with an account of the *genealogy* of Jesus; Luke refers to 'those who *from the beginning* were eyewitnesses and servants of the word' as well as to his own personal investigations '*from the very first*' (Luke 1:2, 3); finally, John takes us to the beginning of all beginnings, the time before the creation.[23]

In reality, of course, each gospel only creates an *impression* of originality – just as every narrative is, of necessity, secondary. In the beginning, there was no story about Jesus – be that story Mark's, Peter's, or anyone else's – but only Jesus himself and the words he spoke.

Historically, before written gospel narratives monopolized the presentation of the good news, sayings attributed to Jesus were transmitted as independent, individual *logoi*. These *sayings traditions*, as scholars now call them, also contained words received from the risen Lord by early Christian prophets.[24] In the course of time, the traditions were compiled into collections, *sayings gospels*, such as the lost gospel 'Q' that the majority of scholars believe was among the sources of Matthew and Luke, and the gospel of Thomas, whose Coptic translation was found in Nag Hammadi, Egypt, in 1945.

---

[23] Cf. Aichele 1996, 39.
[24] For a comprehensive study in early Christian prophecy, see Aune 1983. Several scholars have suggested a close association of the Sayings Gospel Q with early Christian prophecy (thus e.g. Steck 1967, 286–89; Käsemann 1969, 82–107, 108–37; Schulz 1972, 165–75; Edwards 1976, 44–57; Boring 1982, 137–82).

In a way, the sayings format made a claim of authenticity that was one degree stronger than that presented by the narrative gospels. In direct discourse, as opposed to narrative, Jesus was continuously present and addressed every new audience directly. Like the voice of the Divine Wisdom – with whom many early proponents of the sayings traditions apparently identified him – Jesus' words were the same yesterday, today and tomorrow.

The narrative gospels, in turn, bore witness to Jesus' *absence*: Jesus resides *elsewhere*, that is, in the historical past, in the story and, after the end of story, in heaven.[25] In the end, the secret of the kingdom – in other words, a story that claims to have revealed the truth – proves to be an empty sign; appearing to signify insidership, it bears no proper content. 'The truth is out there.'

As if in self-defense, Mark refuses to recognize the primacy of the spoken word. In his narrative, he declares that Jesus' words are enigmas that will only make sense if interpreted. Having thus established that Jesus' speech in fact consisted of signs, Mark transforms Jesus' voice into writing and deconstructs what first seemed an essential difference between his own work and the sayings traditions.[26] Jesus is irrevocably absent, and all that is left are stories.

In Jesus' absence, the only thing present is the narrative itself. In Jesus' silence, it is the task of the narrative to address the reader and to build hermeneutic links between the narrative world and the world of the reader. Today, such links include the languages of literary realism and literary modernism. In this sense, Mark's story has apparently turned out a success.

At the same time, it is important to observe that the form of the narrative still incorporates and gives a material appearance to ideological interpretation. This symbiotic relationship not only determined the original production of the narrative, it also continues to characterize its reception in the present. Even when its impact on its readers apparently has to do exclusively with its poetic properties – its authentic way of representing reality, or the haunting ambiguity of its figurae – the neutrality of this impact is illusory. Authoritative, transcendent reality is still implied – indeed, proclaimed – by means of continuous suggestion of its absence.

---

[25] Cf. Kelber 1983; Syreeni 1988.
[26] Cf. Moore 1992.

4

'Do You Understand what You are Reading?'

In modern literary theory, the concept of the *implied reader* is applied in support of a distinction that separates what is 'in the text' (as the subject of formal analysis) from how the text is interpreted in the light of 'extrinsic' factors, including ideology (as studied by other methods).[1] By postulating a reader typology whose operations can always be traced back to the potential found within the text itself, it becomes possible (or so it is assumed) to account for the reader's presence without having to transcend the limits of textual analysis.

In this chapter, I will use the 'implied reader' concept for somewhat heterodox purposes, with a view to questioning whether such a sharp distinction of intratextual and extratextual aspects is not problematic after all – especially since it concerns aspects of ideological interpretation, and especially as it is applied to narratives composed for ideological purposes, such as the gospels. I hope to be able to show that the implied readers of the gospels are essentially ideological beings; that this makes them profoundly historical beings whose textuality expresses a particular historical experience and social meaning, and thus cannot be grasped as separate from these; and that, most importantly, when used as an interpretive medium that is supposed to determine the ways a text can make sense (so that we might prefer certain readings and interpretations to others), the very concept of the implied reader itself is also both historical and ideological. All this, I believe, is involved in the innocent-looking question 'Is it true that narrative criticism "interprets the texts of the gospels from the point of view of their own implied readers?"'[2]

---

[1] An obvious counterpart to Wayne Booth's concept of the implied author (see Booth 1961), the term implied reader was introduced by Wolfgang Iser (see Iser 1974 [1972]). Subsequently, both concepts have become part of Seymour Chatman's influential theory of narrative as a system of communication (see Chatman 1978).

[2] Powell 1990, 88–89.

Few Things Are Necessary

What would be a *natural* way to read biblical texts? This question is not new, nor is the rivalry, typically ignited by this question, between a 'literalist' or 'first-order' reading on the one hand, and a 'deep' or 'close' reading on the other. As early as in the second century, there was a fervent debate concerning this issue between two famous rabbinical schools of exegesis, namely the schools of Aqiba and Ishmael. To quote Burton Visotzky's paraphrase:

> For Rabbi Ishmael, 'the Torah speaks in human discourse' – that is, Scripture is subject to the same redundancies and occasional verbiage that we all encounter in desultory conversation. Rabbi Aqiba is represented as adamantly opposed to Ishmael's point of view. If Scripture is the Word of God, then no word is superfluous. Every repetition and redundancy bears special meaning. This view is carried so far, in later midrash, that individual letters and even parts of letters are subject to exegesis![3]

In modern critical discussion, the concept of the implied reader refers to the type of adequate response presupposed by a text. Thus, the implied reader of a narrative with, say, lengthy quotations in the Russian language knows Russian. In the case of the gospels, the use of formulae like 'it is written' likewise implies that the reader will recognize this as 'an invocation of biblical authority.'[4]

The type of implied reader the critic thinks the gospels have will affect the way that critic interprets certain features of these narratives. It is, for example, characteristic of the gospels that new episodes open, develop and close abruptly; new characters pop up out of the blue; new settings are introduced without transition. Typically, one of the most common words in the gospel of Mark is εὐθύς, 'suddenly,' or 'immediately.'

What kind of reader does this type of storytelling imply? Two possibilities spring to mind. First, we may argue that the narrator prefers to tell the story in an unexpected way, so that the implied reader will repeatedly be taken by surprise. Alternatively, the implied reader may not be surprised at all, but may regard the gospel's style of narration as natural and unproblematic.

Many narrative critics prefer the first alternative. One typical example is Elizabeth Struthers Malbon who discusses the implied reader of Mark's

---

[3] Visotzky 1996, 17.
[4] Malbon 1996, 100.

gospel in her 'narrative commentary.'[5] For Malbon, Mark's story involves many unexpected turns. As early as in Mark 1:2, she suggests, the implied reader is surprised to hear Isaiah's prophecy and John's story instead of Jesus'. Not long after this, the abruptness of the way the disciples are introduced makes the implied reader puzzled.[6]

Then again, might it not be the case that the implied reader of Mark's gospel is not troubled by the kind of spontaneous storytelling that is peculiar to its implied author? In this case, the novelty of the phrase 'the Son of Humanity' on the lips of Jesus would not – contrary to Malbon's position – strike the implied reader at all, nor would the implied reader be surprised to hear that John had disciples.[7] Rather, he would be well-informed enough to know these things beforehand, or simply accustomed to a way of storytelling in which secondary (or sometimes even truly significant) details may be added as it goes on.[8]

In this latter interpretive scenario, it is indeed a salient characteristic of the Markan implied reader that he has little interest in trivial details – the 'redundancies and occasional verbiage' characteristic of Rabbi Ishmael's 'Torah as human natural discourse.' He does not engage in a 'deep' or 'close' reading that regards everything in the text as weighty and meaningful, but rather reminds us of the implied readers of such functional, goal-oriented forms of storytelling as the joke, the television commercial – and, as Rabbi Ishmael would say, the Hebrew Scriptures. In all these cases, the storyteller keeps with what is necessary and avoids what would be superfluous. The implied reader, of course, is supposed to do likewise. Consider the example given by the playwright David Mamet:

> 'Two guys go into a farm house. An old woman is stirring a pot of soup.' What does the woman look like? What state is the farm house in? Why is she stirring soup? It is absolutely not important. The dirty-joke teller is tending toward a punch line and we know that he or she is only going to tell us the elements which direct our attention toward that punch line, so we listen attentively and gratefully.[9]

---

[5] Malbon 1996.
[6] Malbon 1996, 100, 104.
[7] Malbon 1996, 110, 112.
[8] Considering the androcentrism of Mark's time, I presume the implied reader of the gospel is masculine.
[9] Mamet 1994, 118.

From the point of view of the implied reader (or implied audience), then, the joke is not to be interrupted in order to untangle questions that are 'absolutely not important.' Nor will the implied audience of a commercial presentation ask whether, say, it is truly credible that the girl leaves with a complete stranger just because he is wearing such pleasant after-shave (which is, of course, just as believable as four fishermen suddenly giving up their occupation and leaving their family just because a perfect stranger tells them to do so)?

Thus, the Markan implied reader would not ask 'where the deuce did those scribes (or Jesus' family) pop out of?' in Mark 2:6 (or 3:21), or 'now who initiated this controversy about not fasting in the first place?'[10] Instead, he would be swift to grasp what is of importance: the point of the story, as epitomized in a simple iconic episode, one in a series.

A comparison of the gospels (which many modern biblical critics would regard as popular culture) with (other) forms of popular culture is illuminating. The terse, functional, iconic episodes typical of the narration rather closely match the modern theoretical idea of the *narrateme*, little scenic and narrative epitomes preferred by popular cultural discourse to the 'connotative complexity' and 'polysemic wealth' of high cultural discourse.[11] In the light of this, a 'deep' or 'close' reading of the gospels might imply the posing of questions which could be considered trivial in the context of the narratives themselves.

On the other hand, this is only true in terms of a 'deep' or 'close' reading in the aesthetic, or 'literary' sense of the word. Symbolic, spiritual readings that later became dominant are an entirely different matter. It is to this that I will turn next.

Reading with Understanding

In historical terms, it was not Rabbi Ishmael but Rabbi Aqiba who won the day. On the Christian side, the Alexandrine school of allegorical interpretation overcame the literalist exegetes of Antioch. 'There is nothing in the Scripture superfluous,' says Origen; 'In the divine Scriptures every word, syllable, accent and point is packed with meaning,'

---

[10] *Contra* Malbon 1996, 109, 112, 119.
[11] Cf. Easthope 1991, 94. This, of course, relates closely to the issue of literary value, because popular culture is regularly defined as a negation of 'literature proper.'

says Jerome.[12] Natural or not, Scriptures became texts whose assumed 'polysemic wealth' and 'connotative complexity' would be beyond comparison in history.

However – and this is important – this polysemy is not of an aesthetic kind. While it may become manifest in literary forms, it nevertheless resides on an entirely other, symbolic or ideological level. Although it remains possible, from a typically modern point of view that regards polysemy as a major aesthetic virtue, to read this level of meaning as (if it were) literary, this type of reading (that is, an *aesthetization of ideology*) is not an authentic one and may, as I will attempt to show at the end of this chapter, take place for reasons that are themselves ideological.[13]

What the rabbis and church fathers did was to distinguish between the literal (or 'carnal'), and the 'deep' (or 'spiritual') meanings of the text. The plain, literal sense remained important as such. This was because, as the rabbis and fathers saw it, it bore witness to events of sacred history, since these had once taken place in actual reality. At this 'ordinary,' historical level of meaning, however, it made little difference if the text was sacred or profane. What made the Scripture special was that on a deeper, spiritual level, the holy text was taken to be a mystery that contained a virtually infinite amount of secret knowledge, accessible by means of interpretation.

In anthropological terms, this is not an unusual view of a holy text at all. On the contrary, it is hard to imagine a human community that would not know the idea that divine speech may have a double meaning. Inspired discourse is generally taken to require inspired interpretation; it is the task of holy men and women everywhere to interpret signs and oracles.

Nor is this idea alien to the biblical texts themselves. New Testament writers seek access to the real, spiritual meaning of the Old Testament text by reading it in the light of the christological kerygma. Moreover, many paradigmatic New Testament passages explicitly speak of a correct, *understanding* way of reading and listening, or portray model readers and listeners in action. Other passages show certain characters in a tragicomic light due to the failure of these characters to interpret correctly the message they have received. In all these passages, the key point is

---

[12] Cf. Visotzky 1996, 18.
[13] Cf. Syreeni 1995, 330.

that we should not be fooled by appearances, but understand that what we hear or see is a mystery.

One such paradigmatic passage, perhaps the most paradigmatic of all, is the Markan Parable Theory:

> When he (Jesus) was alone, those who were around him along with the twelve asked him about the parables. And he said to them, 'To you has been given the secret of the kingdom of God, but for those outside, everything comes in parables; in order that
> "they may indeed look, but not perceive,
> and may indeed listen, but not understand;
> so that they may not turn again and be forgiven"' (Mark 4:10–12).

As Frank Kermode has pointed out, the Markan Parable Theory contains, in a nutshell, a general paradigm of all institutionalized interpretation of canonical texts, whether they be part of a canon of holy texts or a canon of literature.[14] As a paradigm of interpretation, the Parable Theory includes three important aspects. First, it establishes a distinction between the carnal and spiritual senses of the text: Jesus' parables are *riddles* that contain more than meets the eye. Second, the Parable Theory implies that the true, spiritual sense of the text can be attained only by means of interpretation. How this takes place is shown in practice when Jesus expounds his Parable of the Sower to his disciples (4:13–20). Third, the Parable Theory makes it clear that the key to correct interpretation is given to an institution, so that no real understanding is possible outside this institution. The reason why Jesus speaks in riddles is that 'those outside' will not understand the true meaning of his words. The truth is for the insiders only.

This is, indeed, how a great deal of biblical interpretation and interpretation of literature works. Once a community of critics has concluded that certain texts need to be interpreted by means of various critical methods, the plain, literal sense of these texts ceases to be sufficient. This turns texts, Mark's gospel and James Joyce's *Ulysses* alike, into enigmas that never stop calling for fresh solutions. Different critics may try different keys to a solution – historical background, universal structures of meaning, the theory of psychoanalysis – but the task itself, the quest for a hidden, deeper meaning, remains the same in all cases. As Jesus puts it (according to Mark): 'There is nothing hidden, except

---

[14] See Kermode 1979, esp. chaps I–III (pp. 1–73).

to be disclosed; nor is anything secret, except to come to light' (Mark 4:22).

Passages like the Parable Theory would seem to further qualify what the implied reader of the gospels should be like. Not only must he not ask trivial, unimportant questions that have nothing to do with the point of the text, but he must also realize that the point of the text can be understood only in a particular interpretive framework. In the story of the gospels, much of what Jesus says and does only makes sense in relation to Old Testament prophecies and the early Christian proclamation about the identity and resurrection of Jesus (and, on the other hand, the true meaning of the Old Testament prophecies as well as the proclamation of Jesus' resurrection only become conceivable in light of the words and deeds of Jesus, as presented in the gospels). Thus, the implied reader should realize that, in order to truly understand what he is reading, he needs to become an insider or seek an insider's guidance. His situation is aptly portrayed in the story of Acts 8:26–40 – another paradigmatic story of how to read a holy text:

Then an angel of the Lord said to Philip, 'Get up and go toward the south to the road that goes down from Jerusalem to Gaza.' (This is a wilderness road.) So he got up and went. Now there was an Ethiopian eunuch, a court official of the Candace, queen of the Ethiopians, in charge of her entire treasury. He had come to Jerusalem to worship and was returning home; seated in his chariot, he was reading the prophet Isaiah. Then the spirit said to Philip, 'Go over to this chariot and join it.' So Philip ran up to it and heard him reading the prophet Isaiah. He asked, 'Do you understand what you are reading?' He replied, 'How can I, unless someone guides me?' And he invited Philip to get in and sit beside him. Now the passage of the scripture that he was reading was this:

'Like a sheep he was lead to the slaughter,
and like a lamb silent before its shearer,
so he does not open his mouth.
In his humiliation justice was denied him.
Who can describe his generation?
For his life is taken away from the earth.'

The eunuch asked Philip, 'About whom, may I ask you, does the prophet say this, about himself or about someone else?' Then Philip began to speak, and starting with this scripture, he proclaimed to him the good news about Jesus. As they were going along the road, they came to some water; and the eunuch said: 'Look, here is water! What is to prevent me from being baptized?' He commanded the chariot to stop, and both of them, Philip and the eunuch, went down into the water, and Philip baptized him. When they came up out of the water, the Spirit of the Lord snatched Philip away; the eunuch saw him no more, and went on his way rejoicing. But Philip found himself at Azotus, and as he was passing through the region, he proclaimed the good news to all towns until he came to Caesarea.

The Ethiopian is a fine example of a *paradigmatic character* typical of the Lukan narrative, of which the Acts is a part.[15] He sets up a standard for the Christian reader to follow. In this particular case, the standard is a standard of reading. In the story, it is established as follows.

First, the Ethiopian is not satisfied with what meets the eye: the mere aesthetic effect of the beautiful and strangely appealing text is not enough for him. Instead, he longs for understanding.

Second, he realizes that understanding is only possible by gaining access to the way insiders read: 'How can I understand, unless someone guides me?' When he learns the true meaning of the text, he immediately asks recognition for his new status as an insider: 'What is to prevent me from being baptized?' Once Philip grants him a new identity, he is able to make it on his own. The Spirit calls Philip to other duties, and the Ethiopian goes 'on his way rejoicing.'

Besides presenting a situation that features an exemplary reader, the narrative is also designed so as to force its own readers to realize how much they, too, depend on inside information. The relationship between Philip and the Ethiopian is very much an image of the relationship between the narrator and the readers. The Ethiopian and the readers face similar challenges in a similar order. First, the narrator lets the readers know what the Ethiopian is reading: the narrative displays the passage of Isaiah in full. Then, in the story, the narrator has Philip ask the Ethiopian about the text: 'Do you understand what you are reading?' Implicitly, the narrator is asking the readers exactly the same question. He requires the readers to know the correct interpretation, just as the passage of Isaiah provided Philip with an occasion to proclaim the good news. How this took place, however – that is, what the real meaning of the passage would be for any reader who understood it – is supposed to go without saying. In other words, the narrative contains an information gap that the readers are supposed to fill. Those who know how to fill it can consider themselves insiders.

[15] On the paradigmatic nature of Lukan characters, see Syreeni 1991; Darr 1992, 1993, 1994.

Those who do not know how to fill it must consider themselves out-siders.[16]

Significantly, the story of Philip and the Ethiopian denies the textual autonomy of Isaiah's prophecy. Apparently – so the narrative implies – reading the Scripture with no other previous knowledge than what the text itself allows takes the reader nowhere. Furthermore, a particular reading competence is required: the Ethiopian cannot understand what he is reading unless an insider guides him.[17] Ultimately, the same goes for the reader of the Lukan narrative as well. He should be familiar with the Jewish Scriptures, their interpretation, and the Christian procla-mation. This, of course, is something that the narrative quite explicitly assumes in its very opening: it is written so that the reader 'may know the truth concerning the things *about which you have been instructed*' (Luke 1:4). Similar references to the implied reader's ideological knowledge of how to read are inherent everywhere in the gospels.[18]

While the Ethiopian is a positive model of an understanding reader, the gospels bristle with negative examples of those who fail to under-stand. As I have mentioned before, the disciples' notorious lack of understanding is a central theme in Mark's narrative. As such, it relates closely to the Markan Parable Theory, because the disciples are the insiders who, in principle, should be familiar with the 'secret of the kingdom.' The fact that they, of all people, fail to understand Jesus is particularly striking.

The so-called *Johannine misunderstandings* provide us with yet another classic set of negative models. In simple terms, the Johannine

---

[16] In all probability, the gap should be filled with what the narrator has previously presented as 'the central content of the Scriptures,' that is, 'that the Christ should suffer and rise from the dead' (παθεῖν τὸν χριστὸν καὶ ἀναστῆναι ἐκ νεκρῶν, Luke 24:46; cf. v. 26). On this basis, the quotation from Isaiah has been selected' (Conzelmann 1987 [1972], 68).

[17] Conzelmann puts this in an insightful way: 'The eunuch asks the questions which the ideal non-Christian Bible reader *should* ask, but which only the Christian reader *can* ask' (Conzelmann 1987 [1972], 69).

[18] In a way, the gospels' intertextual dependency on the Old Testament text on the narrative content level, and the ideological competence that the gospels imply their readers should have, make an apt image – a type, as it were – of the role intertextuality and literary competence play at the formal level of all literary texts. One cannot read a text without being familiar with certain codes based on an effect of *déjà-lu*, the 'already-read,' that is, the reader's (and, of course, the writer's) experience of other literature. (The term *déjà-lu* was introduced by Roland Barthes in Barthes 1974 [1970]; on the notion of *literary competence*, see Culler 1975, 113–130).

misunderstandings consist of one typical scene that is repeated over and over again in the Fourth Gospel.[19] The key element of this scene, in all its variations, is the confusion of the literal and the spiritual sense: people think that Jesus is speaking of earthly things when, in fact, he is speaking of the heavenly (John 3:12). What results is a comic, often grotesque effect, while the character who commits the misunderstanding is shown in an ironic light. In the case of the Johannine misunderstandings, to call the literal sense 'carnal' would be particularly appropriate, because many of the Johannine metaphors relate, in one way or another, to the human body. This is the case when Jesus in John 3:3 says to Nicodemus, 'no one can see the kingdom of God without being born from above,' and Nicodemus answers: 'How can anyone be born after having grown old? Can one enter a second time into the mother's womb and be born?' Elsewhere in the gospel, Jesus speaks of his body as a temple, and as bread; of death as sleep; of water, food and freedom in a spiritual sense; of his mysterious personal knowledge of Abraham; of the mystery of immortality that his words contain; of the mystery of his going away. Each time a failure to see beyond the literal, apparent meaning of Jesus' words leads the hearers astray. Later, Peter does not understand why Jesus wants to wash his feet. Philip cannot see how Jesus could be 'in the Father and the Father in Jesus.' Jesus' kingship is a mystery to Pilate. Mary mistakes the risen Jesus for the gardener. Indeed, Jesus has come 'into this world for judgment so that those who do not see may see, and those who do see may become blind' (John 9:39).

Like the implied reader of Mark, and the implied reader of the Acts, so the implied reader of John is a genuine *apocalyptist* in the very literal sense of the word. He sees that the plain, literal sense is a curtain that hides the truth. To see the truth requires that the curtain be removed by means of interpretation. To master interpretation requires an insider's identity, that is, personal experience of what the Johannine Jesus speaks about: rebirth in baptism, immortality in the Eucharist, guidance in the Spirit. Thus, in the world of the gospels, Christian social experience and identity become necessary preconditions for understanding the narrative.

In a typically biblical view, then, what makes the biblical narrative valuable is not what you see in it – that is, its immanent aesthetic

---

[19] On the role of the Johannine misunderstandings as implicit commentary in John, see Culpepper 1983, 152–165.

properties – but what you do not. Narrative appears as a *code* for the ideology that is its real subject matter. The implied reader possesses a key that can break this code.

Politics of Text, Politics of Reading

It is highly significant that a principally formal, textual analysis of the New Testament gospels should reveal their implied readers to be thoroughly ideological beings. In an equally significant manner, it is in the very desire to assume the implied reader's position and point of view that the essential ideology of narrative criticism becomes exposed (although, as it also turns out, this desire somewhat openly contradicts another earnest wish of narrative critics, namely the wish to focus exclusively on the formal properties of the narrative's internal story-world; such a focus is definitely not the point of view of the implied readers of the gospels, nor has it – as we will see – been the actual point of view in narrative criticism).

Ever since the narrative-critical method was first introduced, it has been warmly welcomed by many critics 'who have been uncomfortable with the challenges posed by historical criticism.'[20] These critics have cherished the 'apparent compatibility between the goals of narrative criticism and the interests of believing communities,' as well as the fact that 'by focusing on the finished form of the text narrative criticism seeks to interpret Scripture at its canonical level.' From their point of view, 'such scepticism [as demanded by historical investigation] is a far cry from the certainty of faith with which the gospel narratives appear to have been written and with which they obviously expect to be read;' luckily enough, '*by interpreting texts from the point of view of their own implied readers, narrative criticism offers exegesis that is inevitably from a faith perspective.*'[21]

We may ask, however, whether it really is this 'faith perspective' that makes narrative criticism so attractive to those not pleased with historical-critical exegesis. In reality, the faith of the implied readers of the early Christian gospels hardly comes too close to the private, individualistic and doctrinal faith of 20th-century Christians. Facing this (historical)

---

[20] Powell 1990, 88.
[21] Powell 1990, 88–89 (my italics); at this point, Powell is strongly criticized by Moore 1994, 115–116.

difference might easily be just as painful as accepting the scepticism required by the historical approach.

A more likely reason for conservative Christians to prefer narrative criticism to a historical approach has been the strong aesthetic emphasis of the former, its promise to center on the poetic aspect of the gospels and leave aside conclusions which might concern the history, doctrine or policies of the Church. The very promise to ignore every ideological aspect would make the approach useful ideologically. This is, after all, exactly what made New Criticism a success story in the America of the 1930s, 1940s and 1950s.

Paradoxical as it is, New Criticism's exclusive focus on the inherent, formal features of literary works had inevitable political implications. The New Critics became associated with political conservatives who likewise thought art should concentrate on 'artistic' issues instead of giving attention to such 'political' matters as poverty and social unrest or, much worse, getting involved in (implicit or explicit) protests against the *status quo*. From the time of the Great Depression and the New Deal, the U.S. government's official cultural policy was to support the 'politically indifferent' current of modernism (the mirror image of the ideals of New Criticism) at the expense of the socially more critical current of realism. Correspondingly, New Criticism assumed the status of a norm for literary criticism in America. 'Artistic' matters were far from being purely artistic. Art that claimed to be indifferent and criticism that claimed to be objective really supported the *status quo*.[22]

It is rather obvious that the originally new-critical ideas about the unity and autonomy of literary works would attract conservative Christians. Vincent B. Leitch speaks of a congruence between fundamentalist Protestant exegesis and the new-critical 'close reading.' In Leitch's view, New Criticism built upon the tradition of fundamentalist hermeneutics that, 'unlike the 'higher criticism' of modern biblical scholarship with its attention to historical matters and textual flaws, conferred divine status on the work and then proceeded worshipfully

---

[22] In the Soviet Union, of course, another type of political interest supported other types of art and criticism. Socialist art was intentionally political and realistic, which is to say that realism came to be the only 'artistic method' that was accepted. From a Marxist point of view, all true art needed to be aware of its connections to prevailing social and historical circumstances. The circle became complete as the East European dissident artists, revolting against the official Marxist views, took the nonchalant playfulness of 'reactionary' and 'degenerated' modernism as a symbol of freedom, creativity and resistance.

to unravel the text.'[23] If the New Critics put the principles of funda-mentalist hermeneutics in a new guise, it is only natural that yet another recycling of these ideas would attract conservative Christians today.

Nor is it much of a surprise that historical critics should become worried. From their point of view, a mere analysis of the formal features of texts as such falls far short of what is required for understanding those texts as writings that have been shaped by the ideas, attitudes and conditions of a particular historical moment. Criticism threatens to be neutralized into an ahistorical praxis which, besides showing suspicious ignorance of its own historical and ideological conditions, could hardly avoid violating its subject of study, the text. Such 'literary' readers who inadvertently assimilate the *storyworld* of the gospels into the symbolic universe (ideology) of their authors or readers not only fail to understand both, but also make less than adequate formal analyses.[24]

As unfortunate as it is for anyone who hopes for politically indifferent exegesis, however, most narrative critics today would hardly keep away from matters beyond the 'purely artistic.' On the contrary, especially in recent years, many of them have become exceedingly involved in matters such as feminism, and the cause of the politically, racially and economi-cally oppressed, as well as in different types of theology of liberation.[25] The way David Rhoads concludes his recent analysis of Mark's *standards of judgment* – that is, the values and beliefs that implicitly govern the narrative world – is a fine case in point:

> Down through history, the standards of the gospel of Mark have been reflected in ordinary folk who have lived courageous lives of service for others. Markan Christians are represented by the orders of the church that called people to give up their livelihood and security to preach the gospel or care for the poor and the ill. Countless missionaries who have left home and country to bring the gospel to remote parts of the world belong in the Markan trajectory. In modern times, their numbers will include those who risked their lives to rescue Jews in Nazi Germany. And we might point to all who joined Martin Luther King in the struggle for civil rights. Most recently, we can point to

---

[23] Leitch 1988, 33.

[24] Cf. Syreeni 1995; see also pp. 122–123 below.

[25] In fact, a similar increase of interest in ideological issues and in the ethics of reading and interpretation characterizes much of recent literary study – including narratology, where several studies in 'ethical criticism of narrative' or 'an ethically oriented method of narratological analysis' have been produced (see e.g. Booth 1988, Rabinowitz 1987, Toker 1993 and Phelan 1996).

the sanctuary movement in this country, the base communities in Latin America, and the struggle of blacks in South Africa. In all nations, where people take courageous risks to bring life to others in the face of persecution, we find Markan Christians.[26]

Now that is hardly a politically neutral perspective on Mark's narrative, nor is it blind to the shared historicity of the text and its interpreters.

In fact, narrative criticism has hardly ever been restricted to a mere structural analysis of the gospel narratives, or to the simple descriptive question 'how do the gospels work?' From the very beginning, it has entered the arena of interpretation and made ideological judgments about the values and beliefs that those narratives promote. Such readings necessarily involve material (and, optionally, spiritual) realities beyond the narrative's exclusive story-world. Very much like the implied readers of the gospels, these readings gaze back on history and prepare for action in the present.

*

Analyzing the implied reader of the gospels turned out to be a trip along a Moebius strip: what began as a study in poetics soon turned into a treatment of ideology. But exactly what kind of form does the relationship between textual features and ideology in the gospels take? What would be productive ways of assessing and organizing it? It is now time to take a closer look at these questions, first by means of practical analysis, then by considering the kinds of broader methodological paradigm this might imply.

[26] Rhoads 1993, 367.

Part II

5

Gaps and Ambiguity in Mark's Narrative Rhetoric

Will a gospel tell us all we need to know in order to understand the good news? Is there anything of importance in the story that we are supposed to infer by ourselves? Or does the good news rather remain ambiguous; is, in the poet's words, 'the longing for news the only news that makes it through?'

Again, Mark's gospel would seem to provide us with a fine test case. It has a reputation for being an enigmatic narrative, bristling with gaps and ambiguity. Secrecy is one of its main themes. On the other hand, one would expect its ideological aims to set a limit on its ambiguity. How do these two sides of Mark combine in a single narrative? In this chapter, I will approach this question by applying insights that originate in some early contributions to the narratological analysis of the Hebrew Bible.

On the Ambiguity of Biblical Narratives

In a 1968 article, 'The King Through Ironic Eyes: Biblical Narrative and the Literary Reading Process,' two members of the so-called Tel Aviv School of Poetics, Menakhem Perry and Meir Sternberg, discussed the phenomenon of textual interplay between alternative reading possibilities that they called a 'multiple system of gap-filling.' As an example of this kind of system they presented the biblical narrative of David and Bathsheba.[1]

According to Perry and Sternberg, the narrator of 2 Samuel 11:1–12 takes an ironic attitude towards King David. He tells the events of the story very briefly, in a seemingly objective way, avoiding comments of any kind. Consequently, the evaluation is left to the readers who, by

---

[1] The article was first published in the Hebrew language (*Ha-Sifrut* 1:2, 263–292). The English version appeared in *Poetics Today* 7:2 (1986), 275–322.

making sense of the information presented to them, gradually come to see David in an increasingly negative light. In other words, the narrator makes use of a particular system of gap-filling in narration.

Part of the distinctive design of the story is that David's character seems to contain somewhat different (if in any case negative) features, depending on whether we believe that Uriah knew of his wife's infidelity and pregnancy or not, and whether we believe that David knew that Uriah knew. According to Perry and Sternberg, a great deal of the narrative's power as literary art is based on the fact that the reader is forced to hesitate between the two alternative reading possibilities, and has to develop more than just one picture of the relationship between the two protagonists in the story. This makes the literary work richer and fuller than it would be if the text were read and realized according to one possible reading hypothesis only.

Sternberg has since written extensively on the poetics of biblical narrative. His key point is that the aim in biblical narrative is to 'reconcile the claims of art and ideology into a happy ideological art.'[2] He sees the poetics of biblical narrative as involving creative interplay between 'the truth' and 'the whole truth.' By 'the truth' he means the elementary minimum information which is necessary for the readers to be given in order that they may understand the narrative's basic intentions correctly. In biblical narratives, 'the truth' is at all times fully transparent to every imaginable reader. 'The whole truth,' in turn, includes matters which the narrator can hide from the reader, for the sake of the fine art of storytelling, in order to entice the reader to make guesses and propose alternative readings. It is this presence of multiple interpretative options that makes biblical storytelling fascinatingly kaleidoscopic.

Significantly, says Sternberg, biblical storytelling never pursues its artistic interests at the cost of its ideological interests. In spite of its sublime ways of generating ambiguity, the Bible has what he calls 'a foolproof composition.' This means that 'the narrator may play games with the whole truth for the pleasure and benefit of the cunning few, but he must communicate the truth in a fashion accessible to all.'[3] Foolproof composition 'provides for minimum intelligibility,' so that 'even the reader who altogether misses the ambiguity – and with it the ironies, double meanings, psychological insights, verbal design, shifts

[2] Sternberg 1987, 135.
[3] Sternberg 1987, 235.

of position, almost everything of value – will still take the moral point.'[4] 'No matter how readers fill in the gaps – even when they see one possibility of the two or more suggested – David [will come out] in disgrace [in the Bathsheba narrative].'[5]

In Sternberg's view, the ideological transparency of the biblical text grants the text clarity in spite of the gaps which it contains. However, the simultaneous coexistence of ideology and gaps has also been seen as a fundamental reason for the inevitably enigmatic and elusive nature of biblical stories. Erich Auerbach puts the matter this way:

> [T]he stories [of the Bible] are not . . . simply narrated 'reality.' Doctrine and promise are incarnate in them and inseparable from them; for that very reason they are fraught with 'background' and mysterious, containing a second, concealed meaning . . . and therefore they require subtle investigation and interpretation, they demand them. Since so much in the story is dark and incomplete, and since the reader knows that God is hidden God, his effort to interpret it constantly finds something new to feed upon.[6]

Auerbach ties together the sparsity, suggestiveness and ambiguity of the biblical narrative and its claim to reveal divine mysteries. It is this very combination, he concludes, that forces the reader of the Bible ceaselessly to seek new meanings in the text. The biblical narrative demands not to be taken at face value, but to be interpreted.

In the previous chapter, I noted that Frank Kermode has picked up Auerbach's point and used it to illustrate how all canonical works, whether they be holy texts or pieces of literature valued for their artistic merit, eventually turn into enigmas that are taken to require explanation and interpretation. For Kermode, the gospels, and especially the gospel of Mark, are fundamental examples of this 'enigmatic and exclusive character of narrative.'[7] In this regard, the Markan Parable Theory is a paradigmatic text above all others, because it explicitly concludes that Jesus' words only make sense to those who know how to interpret them.

For Sternberg, foolproof composition guarantees the transparency of the biblical narrative. From Kermode's point of view, all narratives, and especially biblical ones, are opaque, no matter who reads them or how. There is some subtle irony involved, when both Kermode and

---

[4] Sternberg 1987, 234.
[5] Sternberg 1987, 55.
[6] Auerbach 1953 (1946), 15.
[7] Kermode 1979, 33.

Sternberg evoke a biblical passage to bring home their point – Kermode, the Markan Parable Theory and Sternberg, Moses' Farewell Speech in Deuteronomy:

> Surely, this commandment that I am commanding you today is not too hard for you, nor is it too far away. It is not in heaven, that you should say, 'Who will go up to heaven for us, and get it for us so that we may hear it and observe it?' Neither is it beyond the sea, that you should say, 'Who will cross to the other side of the sea for us, and get it for us so that we may hear it and observe it?' No, the word is very near to you; it is in your mouth and in your heart for you to observe.
>
> (Deut. 30:11–14)

In Sternberg's view, the difference between Mark's gospel and the book of Deuteronomy implies a fundamental difference between the Hebrew Bible and the Greek New Testament: unlike the gospels, the Hebrew Scriptures are accessible to everyone; they make no distinction between 'insiders' and 'outsiders' in their audience.[8]

Yet even for Mark, things are hardly as simple as they first might seem. Certainly, Kermode has a point in saying that Mark *par excellence* is an enigmatic and ambiguous narrative. Such mysterious Markan themes as 'The Messianic Secret' (that is, Jesus' unexplained need to conceal his true, messianic identity), as well as Jesus' disciples' notorious lack of understanding, are classic enigmas that have bothered readers of Mark for centuries – starting from Matthew and Luke who (so I believe) used Mark's gospel as one of their sources.[9] It is apparent that Matthew and Luke found Mark's 'enigmatic and exclusive' nature troublesome every now and then; so often it happened that what Mark left open Matthew and Luke hastened to close.

If Matthew and Luke failed to understand Mark's work, modern critical scholarship has fared no better. In Heikki Räisänen's words, 'Whoever claims to know precisely what Mark was aiming at with his secrecy theory is probably over-reaching himself.'[10]

On the other hand, Paul Ricoeur's conclusion that the gospels, Mark's gospel included, are essentially 'kerygmatic narratives' that are designed so as to drive home an ideological message, must be considered equally

---

[8] Sternberg 1987, 48–49.
[9] For a review of scholarship as well as comprehensive analysis of these themes, see Räisänen 1990.
[10] Räisänen 1983, 135.

apt.[11] In order to be successfully achieved, this kerygmatic aim requires that the gospels, too, have a 'foolproof composition' which 'provides for minimum intelligibility.' How do these two sides of Mark relate to each other?

Narrative Gaps in the Gospel of Mark

According to Sternberg, a gap is

> a lack of information about the world . . . an event, motive, causal link, character trait, plot structure, law of probability . . . contrived by a temporal displacement . . . The storyteller's withholding of information opens gaps, gaps produce discontinuity, and discontinuity breeds ambiguity.[12]

Sternberg goes on to separate omissions into relevancies ('gaps') and irrelevancies ('blanks'), that is, between what was omitted for the sake of interest and what was omitted for lack of interest.

New Testament source criticism has for long regarded discrepancies and points of discontinuity in Mark's gospel as bearing witness to the fact that the evangelist combined material from different traditional sources. To give an example: most critics would say that Mark 2:6–10, a controversy apophthegm, was secondarily imbedded into a miracle story to form 'an apophthegmatic narrative' in Mark 2:1–12.[13] Given that Mark's gospel is a collage, discrepancies and points of discontinuity as such are, obviously, not yet evidence of meaningful literary design. Yet there are many occasions on which it would seem quite natural to see meaningful interruptions, foreshadowings, echoes or omissions in the text. Such points of temporal displacement create suspense, anticipation, and/or different types of juxtaposition. The interpolation of Mark 2:6–10, for example, creates suspense in the narrative: will the interrupted action proceed? Is Jesus, in spite of the resistance he meets, going to heal the paralytic?

In Mark's gospel, an obvious example of purposeful informational gapping is provided by the request of the Boanerges brothers James and John (10:35–45). Jesus' words 'You do not know what you are asking' indicate a gap: there is more in the request than meets the eye.

[11] See Ricoeur 1990.
[12] Sternberg 1987, 235–236.
[13] Thus e.g. Bultmann 1968 (1931), 209.

Explanation follows: Jesus prophesies that James and John will 'drink the cup that he will drink,' and that they will 'be baptized with the baptism with which he is baptized;' 'but to sit at my right hand or at my left is not mine to grant, but it is for those for whom it has been prepared.' To some extent, the narrator is counting on the reader's competence to solve the riddle and fill the gap; just a few moments previously, Jesus had spoken about his coming death – for the third time in just the past two chapters. A cup is a common symbol of fate in the Orient; a statue of a god or a goddess with the cup of fate in its hands is a standard type.[14] Christian baptism was, from early on, 'a baptism into Christ's death' (cf. Rom. 6:3–4). On the other hand, the gap is closed within the narrative itself. The simile of the cup is re-introduced in the Gethsemane story (Mark 14:36), this time with a clear reference to Jesus' approaching death. In the crucifixion scene, the readers are told that with Jesus 'they crucified two bandits, *one on his right and one on his left*' (15:27).[15]

For a specifically Markan way of programmatic gap-making, we might consider the famous Markan 'sandwiches' or intercalations. Mark has a well-recognized habit of combining two originally non-interdependent narratives by means of different kinds of framing techniques.[16] These framing techniques introduce textual arrangements that distort the linear flow of the narrative in order to get certain events linked with each other in a certain way. As an example (in addition to the case of Mark 2:1–12 mentioned above), consider the narrative presentation of Jesus' Temple demonstration and the Cursing of the fig-tree (11:11–25): two symbolic actions that most likely picture the judgment of Israel[17] are

[14] See also Ps. 11:6; Hab. 2:6; cf. Camery-Hoggatt 1992, 162.

[15] Cf. Tolbert 1989, 31–32; Camery-Hoggatt 1992, 161–162.

[16] Ernst von Dobschütz (1928) was the first to draw attention to this. At the moment, there is no firm scholarly agreement on the exact number of actual 'sandwich-arrangements' in the gospel. The establishment of an exact number is difficult, because several different kinds of framing techniques – often overlapping each other – occur in Mark's gospel (see Dewey 1991, 233). The more or less 'classic' cases, as listed by Frans Neirynck (1988, 133) include Mark 3:20–21(22–30)31–35, 5:21–24(25–34)35–43, 6:7–13(14–29)30–31, 11:12–14(15–19)20–25, 14:1–2(3–9)10–11, and 14:53(54)55–65(66–72). In any case, 'among the evangelists Mark employs the sandwich technique in a unique and pronounced manner' (Edwards 1989, 216). For recent discussion on this subject, see van Oyen 1992.

[17] The most important arguments that support this very popular interpretation are (1) the general context in which the episode appears in Mark 11 and 12: Jesus' prophetic activity in the Temple, ending with the prophecy of destruction in 13:2; and (2) the commonness of the fig-tree as an image of Israel in the Hebrew scriptures. (See Telford 1980.)

presented in between each other, very much in the manner of an early Eisensteinian cinemontage. Significantly, the text does not make the connection between the two events on the content level explicit in any way. It is up to the reader to draw the strings together and read the text complete.

Some words of warning are appropriate, however. First, informational gapping can hardly be considered a clearly discernible, coherent artistic program which would run through the whole of Mark's gospel. In most cases, as it seems, the Markan narrator introduces commentary in a very straightforward manner where it is easiest to add and where it is of greatest immediate relevance. Sometimes meaningful gaps result, sometimes they do not. Compare the two episodes Mark 10:17–22 (Jesus and the rich man) and 12:18–27 (the Sadducees question Jesus about resurrection). In the first episode, the piece of information which is crucial to understanding the whole is given only at the very end of the narrative (the man had many possessions); in the second episode, this piece of information is introduced right at the beginning (the Sadducees say there is no resurrection). It is hardly the most obvious explanation that, on the former occasion, the narrator had a greater need to sustain the reader's interest in the outcome of the story than on the latter. It is rather that the narrator inserts commentary where it fits best: Jesus' words about giving up one's possessions made the potential follower sad, because he had many; the Sadducees, who actually did not believe in the hereafter, asked Jesus a question about the life to come.[18]

Furthermore, much intentional informational gapping must have been present already in Mark's sources – which, in turn, makes it more or less difficult to discuss informational gapping in Mark in any strictly systematic terms. If we think of Jesus' parables, for example, ever since Joachim Jeremias's classic work *Die Gleichnisse Jesu* (1947), it has been generally recognized that, in the process of becoming tradition, parables tend to develop towards a greater degree of explicit explanation, allegorization and interpretative closedness. The more original a tradition, the more it leaves for its reader or hearer to work out; the later the tradition, the more it is the narrator who takes care of the interpretation. This can be well seen by comparing the three synoptic gospels with each other. The story of Jesus and the Syrophoenician woman – a narrative which contains parabolic elements – is a good

---

[18] Against Fowler 1991, 98, 109–110.

example. Mark's version of the story (Mark 7:24–29) leaves it for the reader to make the connection between the sick daughter's ethnic origin and the talk about puppy dogs and little children. Matthew, reading Mark, lets Jesus (in Matt. 15:24) provide the reader beforehand with the necessary interpretative key.[19]

Second, although gaps create ambiguity – momentary or permanent – in the Markan text, ambiguity is, by and large, not what the gospel is aiming at. As we will see, the gospel's narrative rhetoric more or less clearly implies that the gospel is intended to be normative proclamation. As such, the aim is to get a comprehensible message through. If there are riddles in the text, the audience is, in most cases, expected to solve them sooner or later. As the gospel itself puts it: 'there is nothing hidden, except to be disclosed; nor is anything secret, except to come to light' (Mark 4:22).[20] Thus, at least in the cases in which the gaps (or any other formal feature in the gospel) have 'an instrumental relationship to the narrator's theology,'[21] they most certainly are introduced in the text so that the *right* connections will be made. The audience is not expected to produce free alternative readings, but rather to gain a proper understanding of what it means to follow Jesus. At times, the narrator may be willing to run the risk that his most enigmatic tones are not understood, at least not by everyone, but under no circumstances would he be ready to accept being *misunderstood*. In this sense, Mark's narrative, too, strives for genuine 'foolproof composition.'

Mark's Narrative Rhetoric as an Effort towards 'Foolproof Composition'

In recent years, a number of studies have analyzed Mark's narrative rhetoric, in other words the variety of choices and techniques of story-telling that the gospel applies to condition and control the ways its readers read it. On this occasion, I will only give a few examples – as many as are enough to make a point.

Every narrative is a selective reduction of reality. A particular voice tells the story, and a particular pair of eyes focalizes the events. What the readers hear and see depends on who speaks and who sees in the

---

[19] Cf. Fowler 1991, 117 n. 58.
[20] Cf. Kelber 1988, 1.
[21] Cf. Boomershine 1974, 9–30, 261–263, 335.

narrative. In the world of the gospels (as well as biblical narratives in general), *narrators* are mostly anonymous, omniscient third persons who are not bound by time or space. Very much like the God whom they proclaim, they are 'an implied invisible presence in every scene.'[22] Such a narrator can see and tell what in the story takes place behind closed doors or deep in the minds of the *dramatis personae*; the narrator knows the true feelings and the secret motifs of all the characters. This makes him or her able to recount the events from a privileged point of view as compared to that of the characters, or of the reader. The characters and the reader see the outward appearance; the godlike narrator has the ability to look on the heart of matters (cf. 1 Sam. 16:7).

As a case in point, Robert Fowler has analyzed the Markan episode in which Jesus walks on the sea.[23] What is important is the way the narrator makes use of his privileged perceptive point of view. The episode begins with an overall view given from the narrator's perspective: the disciples are in a boat out at sea, Jesus is alone on the land (Mark 6:47). The narrator then provides the reader with an opportunity to see things through Jesus' eyes: he notes that '*Jesus saw* that they (that is, the disciples) were straining at the oars against an adverse wind.' Next, he says that Jesus came towards the disciples, walking on the sea, with the intention to pass them by (so the narrator even knows what Jesus had in mind; 6:48). After this, that is, once the reader *knows* what is happening, he or she is told what the disciples *think* is happening: when the disciples see Jesus walking on the sea, they think it is a ghost and start to cry out loud (6:49). What Jesus now says to the disciples, the reader has known all along: there is nothing to worry about, 'it is I' (6:50). So there is no chance for the reader to identify himself or herself with the disciples, that is, to share with them first the fear and then the relief. This is because that is the way the narrator wants it. The reader is not meant to join the disciples in their mistrust and incomprehension, but to condemn it. In the end, the narrator gives his own harsh judgment on the disciples: they lacked understanding; their hearts were hardened (6:52).

Once the narrator chooses to take sides with his or her audience against the characters, the basis is laid for the occurrence of *irony* in the

---

[22] Rhoads 1982, 420, with reference to Petersen 1978. To be sure, there are occasional exceptions to the rule: at the beginning of the gospel of Luke, and again at the beginning of the Acts of the Apostles, the narrator identifies both himself and his audience; cf. Luke 1:1–4; Acts 1:1; furthermore, the narrative of Acts is partly in the first person.

[23] Fowler 1991, 217.

narrative.[24] In a classic work, *A Rhetoric of Irony* (1974), Wayne C. Booth examines the mocking salute that the Roman soldiers give to Jesus ('Hail, King of the Jews!' in Mark 15:18) as a textbook example. According to Booth, there is irony on two levels in the scene. First, the soldiers intend their salute to be ironic. Second, they themselves are subjected to irony, for little do they know that their mocking words happen to be true, that Jesus really is the Messiah, the King of Israel. Of the first level of irony the characters themselves are well aware; the second level is available only to the readers, who from the first verse of the gospel on have been privileged to know that Jesus is 'Christ, the Son of God.' The audience belongs to the insiders, while the soldiers are outsiders; irony is the narrator's way of showing that, in order to understand, you really have to depend on what the narrator says.[25]

Stressing the need for privileged knowledge on the level of the story, and further demonstrating this need on the level of storytelling, are means by which the Markan narrator makes his readers depend on inside information. Once the readers become dependent on the narrator, the narrator seeks to ensure that the readers at all times have a proper angle to the story. This can take place in a variety of ways, including manipulating the perceptive point of view in the narrative (as was the case in the story of Jesus walking on the sea), as well as through the narrator's implicit and explicit comments on the narrative.

In Mark, the narrator's explicit comments are a particularly strong piece of evidence of the gospel's interest in reducing ambiguity and filling potentially harmful gaps in the narrative even before they open up.[26] In verses 3:2, 12:13, and 14:10, for example, Mark attaches to the description of Jesus' opponents ἵνα-*clauses* that leave very little doubt about their future intentions: καὶ παρετήρουν αὐτὸν εἰ τοῖς σάββασιν θεραπεύσει αὐτόν, ἵνα κατηγορήσωσιν αὐτοῦ (they watched him to see whether he would cure him on the Sabbath, *so that they might accuse him*); καὶ ἀποστέλλουσιν πρὸς αὐτόν τινας τῶν

---

[24] Camery-Hoggatt 1992 presents a comprehensive study on irony in Mark's gospel. Significantly, most of the occasions of irony occur in the Passion Narrative. Fowler (1991, 159) puts it well: 'hardly a word is spoken by any character in the Passion narrative that the reader can take up in a straightforward fashion.'

[25] See Booth 1974, 28–29; cf. Rhoads and Michie 1982, 59–61; Fowler 1991, 11–12; Camery-Hoggatt 1992, 2–4.

[26] Cf. Boomershine 1974, 287. Of course, Mark is still at the beginning of the road in this respect: Matthew and Luke find a great many opportunities to answer questions left unanswered by Mark.

φαρισαίων καὶ τῶν Ἡρῳδιανῶν ἵνα αὐτὸν ἀγρεύσωσιν λόγῳ (then they sent to him some Pharisees and some Herodians *to trap him in what he said*); καὶ Ἰούδας Ἰσκαριὼθ ὁ εἷς τῶν δώδεκα ἀπῆλθεν πρὸς τοὺς ἀρχιερεῖς ἵνα αὐτόν παρπδοῖ αὐτοῖς (then Judas Iscariot, who was one of the twelve, went to the chief priests *in order to betray him to them*).[27] Among particularly salient Markan features are parenthetic *γάρ-clauses* that explain why some character(s) act(s) in a certain way.[28] Eventually, the gospel ends with a double occurrence of such a clause: Καὶ ἐξελθοῦσαι ἔφυγον ἀπὸ τοῦ μνημείου, εἶχεν γὰρ αὐτὰς τρόμος καὶ ἔκστασις · καὶ οὐδενὶ οὐδὲν εἶπαν · ἐφοβοῦντο γάρ. ('So they went out and fled from the tomb, *for terror and amazement had seized them*; and they said nothing to anyone, *for they were afraid*.') Finally, a paradigm case of the lengths to which the Markan narrator is prepared to go to make his narrative foolproof is found in the context of the apocalyptic discourse of Mark 13. There, in verse 14, the narrator suddenly, in the middle of Jesus' speech, speaks directly to the audience: 'But when you see the desolating sacrilege set up where it ought not to be (*let the reader understand*), then those in Judea must flee to the mountains.' Once again, Jesus' words hide a riddle, and the narrator wishes to make this known to anyone who might be reading the text. An understanding reader who has been given access to the secrets of the Kingdom (Matthew certainly was one; cf. Matt. 24:15) would know that 'the desolating sacrilege' refers to the Book of Daniel (Dan. 9:27); the place where it ought not to be is the Temple of Jerusalem. The situation of the Jewish war looms in the background.[29]

---

[27] Cf. Fowler 1991, 101.

[28] Cf. Boomershine 1974, 271; Fowler 1991, 92–98.

[29] Quite a lot of scholars assume that Mark 13:14 has something to do with wartime events in the Temple (although some, namely those who think that the saying originates from a pre-Markan tradition, suggest a different frame of reference for τὸ βδέλυγμα τῆς ἐρημώσεως ἑστηκότα ὅπου οὐ δεῖ; such a frame could be a prophecy about a personal antichrist; Caligula's attempt to have his statue set up in the Temple in 40 CE; Pilate's setting up the imperial standards in Jerusalem in 19 CE; or perhaps a more general type of reference to the Roman Empire as an embodiment of evil; see Collins 1992, 84–85). As to exactly what particular wartime event the text refers, there is no consensus. Some suggest that the βδέλυγμα τῆς ἐρημώσεως refers to the destruction of the Temple as such; the masculine participle ἑστηκότα represents the Roman general or his army (thus e.g. Lührmann 1987, 222). Others claim a more specific reference, e.g. to Titus who, according to Josephus, went into τὸ ἅγιον τοῦ ναοῦ after it had already been set afire (*J. W.* 6.4.7 §260; see Marcus 1992, 454), or to a foreign cultic image that was

71

Thus, it is not only matters inside the story that are to be interpreted in an understanding way. The apocalyptic view on history that makes itself known in Mark 13 suggests that *the entire reality* is a riddle, a collection of signs of the times, waiting for an understanding interpreter who has eyes to see and ears to hear. Just as the leaves on the fig-tree are a sign of the coming summer, so also are war and suffering signs of the end (Mark 13:28–29). Everything is significant; reality as we see it is a riddle.

Transparency vs. Opacity in Mark's Narrative

In *Let the Reader Understand: Reader-Response Criticism and the Gospel of Mark* (1991), Robert Fowler has done remarkable work in giving a systematic presentation of the multitude of ways in which the gospel of Mark attempts to take control over its readers. With reference to this control, Fowler speaks of 'Mark's rhetoric of direction.' 'When its rhetoric of direction is particularly compelling,' Fowler concludes, 'this narrative tells us exactly and unquestionably what to see, hear, understand, think, and believe.'[30] This, however, is not the whole story. In what Fowler calls 'Mark's rhetoric of indirection,' he discovers a very modern and antiauthoritarian side of Mark. In Fowler's view, Mark is also intentionally seeking to 'avoid univocality,' thus 'pressing upon the reader an interpretative freedom, a challenge to respond to the reading experience as we will:' 'Frequently . . . our narrator avoids leading us into any kind of clarity whatsoever . . . [but] pulls the reader so vigorously in different directions simultaneously, that [what results is] ultimately an ambivalent narrative.'[31] After having done so much to uncover the 'clear, determinate, direct and authoritarian' side of Mark, Fowler still

---

again feared to be set in the Temple (thus Collins 1995, 20). I favor Joel Marcus's proposition that the βδέλυγμα τῆς ἐρημώσεως is rather 'the Temple's occupation by various revolutionary leaders beginning in 67 CE – an event which Josephus also describes, in terms echoing Daniel 11:31 and 12:11, as a defilement' (Marcus 1995, 1; a comprehensive presentation of Marcus's thesis can be found in Marcus 1992). Whatever the case, the riddle presented in the Markan text is supposed to provide the Markan audience with an answer to another riddle in their real-life situation: what does the destruction/desecration of the Temple signify as an eschatological event, and how should one react to such a sign?

[30] Fowler 1991, 261.
[31] Fowler 1991, 251, 261; 195.

seems to put the emphasis on the 'ambiguous, opaque, indirect and libertarian' side of the gospel.[32]

How do the ambiguity of Mark's gospel and the Markan narrator's efforts towards a foolproof composition relate to each other? The question is whether these two sides of Mark are really commensurate. It seems to me that, in so far as the gospel hides matters in order that these matters may be disclosed later, or keeps things secret just in order to bring them to light (which, in the Markan view, seems to be the only legitimate type of secrecy there is; cf. Mark 4:22), ambiguity in Mark simply works for the purpose of the narrator's 'rhetoric of direction.' As for those occasions on which ambiguity does not carry this function, on the other hand, the most natural conclusion is that it is purely unintentional in these cases. This, in turn, would make it difficult to speak of any 'rhetoric of indirection' as the Markan narrator's strategy.

It is essential to make a distinction between what is intentional and what is accidental in Mark (and I am not speaking primarily about *the author's* intention here, but rather about what can reasonably be conceived as *the narrator's* strategy). It may be that Fowler does not always give enough attention to this difference. Indeed, at times it seems as if he regards nothing at all in the narrative as accidental – or, in Sternberg's terms, as if all the Markan 'blanks' were 'gaps,' too. Consequently, all textual ambiguities, omissions of information, and points of discontinuity alike are transformed into evidence of the narrator's ingenuity.[33] Moreover, Fowler allows the reader very much interpretative freedom to decide where it is that the text manifests ambiguity or withholds meaningful information, and how.

To give an example: 'In Gethsemane, Peter's failure to stay awake and to maintain the vigil with Jesus is accentuated when Jesus addresses him not with the nickname used consistently since 3:16, but with his old name: ". . . and he said to Peter, 'Simon, are you asleep? Could you not watch one hour?'"' (14:37).[34] Verse 14:37 is the *only* occasion Jesus calls Peter by *any* name (verse 8:33, in which he calls Peter 'Satan,' is

---

[32] Fowler 1991, 261.

[33] This is actually implied in the very use of the term rhetoric. To speak of rhetoric (of direction as well as of indirection) tends to suggest that, in the text, 'signification is always successful and cannot envisage, for example, a Freudian slip except as something deliberately intended' (Easthope 1991, 108).

[34] Fowler 1991, 181–182.

not counted). Jesus' being this personal is, as such, a much bigger anomaly in the framework of the story than his choosing to call Peter 'Simon.' What is accentuated here is how close Jesus and Peter are supposed to be to each other (a theme developed further throughout the story of Jesus' arrest) – which, of course, makes Peter's failure much worse. The point is, that against this background, the use of the name Simon, that is, Peter's actual personal name, is not very problematic. There are not many grounds for asking 'Why is Jesus not calling Peter Peter but Simon?' The gap is not so much in the text as in the eye of the reader who is inclined to find what he is looking for. (Frankly, I cannot help thinking that should Jesus have called Peter 'Peter' at this point, Fowler might just as well have taken this as another manifestation of the verbal irony inherent in the meaning of the name Peter – 'the rock' – in Mark.)

Similarly, when arguing that the centurion's confession in Mark 15:39 is not sincere but must be understood ironically, Fowler asks, 'Have we not already comprehended in our reading the essential qualities of the Roman soldiers, of whom the centurion is probably (we infer) the officer in charge?'[35] Should Fowler have wanted to argue the other way round, he could just as well have said that what we have here is a case of the 'gross incongruity between what the reader expects of [a character] and what [he] actually [does] in the story,' typical of Markan storytelling.[36]

Fowler quite frequently – and often quite rightly – criticizes historically-oriented critics for their eagerness to find a referential explanation for everything in Mark's gospel. The question remains, however, whether Fowler's own attempts to explain everything in the gospel in terms of the narrator's rhetorical strategies are any different. Do not Fowler's more or less all-inclusive rhetorical explanations, too, manifest 'the modern critical spirit yearning for clarity?'[37]

On the whole, we have, I think, enough evidence of the Markan narrator's intention of reducing ambiguity inherent in the narrative. Mark's 'rhetoric of direction' more or less clearly indicates that the narrator's overall goal is to reduce ambiguity, not introduce it. To be sure, much ambiguity still remains; we will have to remember that

---

[35] Fowler 1991, 207.
[36] Fowler 1991, 171.
[37] Fowler 1991, 196.

what is now the story of Mark's gospel was composed out of material which had previously circulated in different traditions, and that Mark the evangelist was the very first person to make a unified narrative out of them. Keeping this in mind, we must keep our expectations of unity and coherence on a reasonable level.[38] Furthermore, even though Mark may have aspired to clarity, his attempts to clear things up were not always successful. Sometimes they may rather have added confusion, as 'the more the narrative strives to reveal, the more it becomes involved in concealments.'[39] Nevertheless, the farther we stray into the area where 'uncertainty dominates' in Mark, the more certainly we are dealing with the accidental and the unintended. These aspects are not aimed at a rhetorical purpose any more than at referential significance. As Perry and Sternberg put it,

> The multiple system of gap-filling must not be equated with confusion, sloppiness or vagueness. Where a text accommodates various gap-fillings merely because certain relevant data happen to be lacking or obscure, and fails to exploit these possibilities in order to impose some artful patterning on the unfolding elements, there is no point in talking about 'interplay' and 'tension' between alternative possibilities.[40]

*

Apart from the unintentional 'blanks' due to the evangelist's use of different traditions, intentional systems of gaps do exist in Mark's gospel. However, the ideological aims of the gospel set a limit on the amount of ambiguity its narrative allows. Even when playing with mystery, secrecy and indirection, the narrator displays ideological interests that give the narrative a serious, monologic tone. What results is a Janus-like narrative where the 'clear, determinate, direct and authoritarian' side nevertheless does its best to take the upper hand.

---

[38] Thus also Räisänen 1990, 33. Räisänen points out that what makes Mark's striving towards unity and coherence particularly difficult is his attempt to fuse together two separate worlds in one single narrative: 'on the one hand, he is telling a story of what happened when Jesus of Nazareth was active in Galilee and in Jerusalem; on the other hand, he is projecting the story of his own Christian congregation onto the same screen. – This duality unavoidably brings a tension – which cannot be resolved if one remains within the 'story world' alone.' (Räisänen 1990, 19.)

[39] Kelber, 1988, 1.

[40] Perry and Sternberg 1986 (1968), 320.

Significantly, it is the very peculiar marriage of poetics and ideology that provides Mark's narrative with both unity and diversity. On the one hand, ideology is the cement that holds the diverse elements and patterns together, thus giving the narrative inherent unity and coherence where it otherwise might turn out fragmentary and disconnected. On the other hand, however, ideology disunites the narrative by turning it into a commentary, that is, by adding an extra voice that requires it not to be taken as it is but rather to be explained and interpreted. Paradoxical as it is, while fiercely calling for an entirely monologic narrative, ideology points out the many voices present in the text. This peculiar dualism is, I think, the very essence of all gospel narratives.

6

Characters in the Making

As far as biblical characterization is concerned, perhaps the most central question of all concerns the *representation of individuality*. In this respect, the mystery of biblical characters is the mystery of the mustard seed: how does so much come out of so little? How do figures who are sketched with only few harsh strokes manage to give an impression of individuality and personhood?

In this chapter, my aim is to show that characterization in the gospels is related to changes that are due to ideological conditions. An attentive reader can detect two opposing lines of development. While some characters become increasingly subtle as Mark's story is retold by Matthew and Luke, others are stripped of their individuality and subjective performance, and are turned into simple agents. Paradoxical as it may seem, the reason behind these changes appears to be the same in both cases: the narrative is striving to become more consistently monologic, which would enhance the ideological naturalization of all its elements. For some characters, this means that their inner emotions, reactions and intentions need to be clarified, so that no misinterpretation on the reader's part will disturb the ideological impact. As a consequence, these characters become 'fuller.' As for some other characters, it is safer to deny them voice and vision altogether. Not surprisingly, the characters most liable to lose their share of narrative subjectivity are those whose actions, words or points of view somehow contest the dominant ideology.

Thus, the characters in the gospels are only in the process of becoming what they are. Rather than being static elements of design picked by a master author to fill a distinct literary or rhetorical purpose, they are constantly being reshaped by distinct ideological dynamics. This ideologically attuned aspect of character presents a challenge for any theory or model of characterization for the gospel narratives.[1] Rigid

---

[1] Certainly, 'character' remains a complicated theoretical issue in its own right; some consider it 'both the most central and the most problematic concept of narrative theory,' even to the extent that 'in the course of the long history of Western criticism and poetics, characters

mechanistic models need to be replaced with more flexible ones that treat the gospels as part of a living, evolving tradition. Because there is 'a relation between ideological dominance and specific forms of representation,' analysis of the ideology should be an integral part of the analysis of the formal features of the narrative.[2] This analysis need not necessarily be neutral. Perhaps the critic might consider the text not so much as an object of formal description, but as a challenge to his or her own personal convictions.[3]

On the Impersonal Nature of Biblical Characterization

Obviously, many characters in the gospels are individuals in the sense that they have, for example, a proper name and a particular setting. Yet their individuality is more or less impersonal: as agents, they remain subordinate to action; as types, they remain subordinate to the more general human (or sometimes superhuman) qualities they exemplify. While, of course, it makes a marked difference whether Jesus heals an anonymous blind person or a close friend named Lazarus, the more distinctive individuality of the latter does not yet make that character much of a personality. Even Jesus himself, the protagonist of the story, is typically characterized as the 'Son of God,' a figure of a particular type, rather than a troubled, thoughtful young Nazarene, as modern literature would have him, for whom fate is not predestined but the result of personal choices.

Indeed, matters could hardly be otherwise. After all, psychological interest in the individual as a personality is a relatively new phenomenon in Western art (just as the individualist idea of identity as selfhood has only emerged with modernity). In antiquity, characters had not so much 'personality' in the modern sense, as *ethos* – a static, unchanging set of virtues and vices.[4]

---

have never been described in a satisfactory way theoretically' (Bal 1987, 3, 105). The classification of characters by their 'fullness' is an essential part of this problem; see e.g. Rimmon-Kenan 1983, 40–42; Bal 1985 (1980), 81.

[2] Bal 1987, 3. In her numerous works of the 1980s, Bal aimed at putting narrative theory at the service of ideology critique, specifically feminism. Significantly, many of these works involved analyses of biblical texts. In addition to Bal 1987 – and its earlier French version (Bal 1986) – see Bal 1988a and Bal 1988b.

[3] Here I take my lead from Todorov 1988, 155–168.

[4] Tolbert 1993, 348–349. For perspectives on characterization and individuality in Greek literature, see Pelling (ed.) 1990.

Even today, economic characterization and the use of simple, recognizable standard types (such as the *femme fatale*, the hypochondriac, or the sage's stupid disciple) remain a practical necessity for all forms of storytelling that are designed to make a simple point: the exemplary, educative or ideological story with a moral – as well as the *joke* whose every single feature is directed towards the punch line. In stories of this kind, character types are most practical, because they give in a condensed form everything the audience needs to know about the figures presented. Any more detailed characterization would be superfluous and disturbing.

Correspondingly, then – and now I am, once more, referring to Erich Auerbach's memorable assessment of Mark's narrative,

> The author of the Gospel according to Saint Mark has no viewpoint which would permit him to present a factual, objective portrait of, let us say, the character of Peter. He is at the core of what goes on; he observes and relates only what matters in relation to Christ's presence and mission; and in the present case [of Peter's denial] it does not even occur him to tell us how the incident ended, that is, how Peter got away . . .[5]

The personal elements are there only in so far as they are necessary to achieve the objective toward which the narrative is tending. In the framework of an individual miracle story, this objective is the occurrence of the miraculous; in a controversy story, it is the final word uttered by the protagonist silencing all objections; in a gospel, it is 'Christ's presence and mission.'

The Role of the Reader in the Making of Biblical Characters

Thus, at least at first glance, ancient literary conventions and the evangelists' ideological objective appear to exclude any particular interest in the individual and the personal. In biblical scholarship, the form critics were quite emphatic about this, and their view remains dominant even today.[6]

On the other hand, a number of literary critics have claimed that, while the (Hebrew as well as the Greek) Bible's sparseness in giving any formal portrayal of characters may be something rather unique even in ancient literature (compare biblical figures with Homeric figures, or

---

[5] Auerbach 1953 (1946), 47.
[6] See Burnett 1993, 9.

those of the Icelandic saga), that very sparseness may result in a more dynamic and personal view of character. This is due to the fact that reticence in characterization invites the reader to play an active part in the making of characters. Given only sparse and ambiguous information, the reader simply has to infer, make guesses and interpretations, and correct those guesses and interpretations whenever his or her expectations are not fulfilled in the course of the narrative. The reading process becomes a drama with lines of development, which in itself conveys a particular (and, it would seem, rather modern) view of the human character as dynamic, full of surprises, and capable of change.

Again, it all returns to ideas first presented by Erich Auerbach. It was originally his grand idea that the retention and suggestiveness of the biblical narrative makes it 'fraught with background:' 'Since so much in the story is dark and incomplete, and since the reader knows that God is a hidden God, his effort to interpret it constantly finds something new to feed upon.'[7] The silence of the text encourages the reader to fill the gaps. Both Robert Alter and Meir Sternberg have developed this idea in relation to characterization in the Hebrew Bible. Interestingly enough, both connect the (quite original, so it seems) strategies used in the rendering of biblical characters with biblical monotheism and the biblical view of humanity.

Sternberg's starting point was his general idea of the biblical narrative as an interplay between 'the truth' and 'the whole truth.' To review, briefly, this idea explained in the previous chapter, 'the truth' consists of the essentials that the narrative makes perfectly clear to every reader on every occasion: the story line, the world order, the value system. 'The whole truth,' in turn, is something the readers have to infer for themselves, filling in what the narrative purposefully leaves untold. The art of biblical narrative is to get the readers involved in a systematic process of gap-filling.

As to biblical characters, there are, according to Sternberg, marked differences between God and humans. In God's case, the narrator's reticence is related to the biblical view of God's qualitative distance from both humans and pagan gods. Only little is told, because there is not much to tell: most dimensions conventionally associated with character (such as physical appearance, social status, personal history, local habitation) simply do not apply to God. Furthermore, information

---

[7] Auerbach 1953 (1946), 15.

is strategically withheld about God *and* human beings so as *to make reading a character a process of discovery*. Before the readers' eyes, the characters take shape gradually, often in unexpected ways, so that there is usually a notable distance between the first impression and the last. All along, the readers play an active part in the process. Because only a partial picture of the character is given, the readers must round it off by their own efforts. Yet again, the qualitative distance between God and humans makes a difference. Whereas God is constant and stable, humans vary and change. While God *is*, humans are only *in the process of becoming* what they are. So while the readers can safely rely on whatever discoveries they make about God in the course of the narrative, they may never be quite sure about biblical men and women.[8]

In a quite similar manner, Robert Alter likes to emphasize the biblical characters' *capacity for change,* which reflects 'a sense of the unknowable and the unforeseeable in human nature.'[9] Ultimately, this brings the biblical characters closer to characters in modern literature than are the heroes of the Greek epics:

> Cognate with the biblical understanding of individual character as some-thing which develops in and is transformed by time – pre-eminently in the stories of Jacob and David – is a sense of character as a center of surprise. This unpredictable and changing nature of character is one reason why biblical personages cannot have fixed Homeric epithets (Jacob is not 'wily Jacob,' Moses is not 'sagacious Moses') but only relational epithets deter-mined by the strategic requirements of the immediate context: Michal, as the circumstances vary, is either 'daughter of Saul' or 'wife of David.' ... the underlying biblical conception of character as often unpredictable, in some ways impenetrable, constantly emerging from and slipping back into a penumbra of ambiguity, in fact has greater affinity with dominant modern notions than do the habits of conceiving character typical of the Greek epics.[10]

Ideas similar to Alter's and Sternberg's have been presented in the context of New Testament scholarship in a recent article by Fred Burnett. Like Alter and Sternberg, Burnett, too, focuses on the reader's role in giving depth to the rather sketchy characters of the gospels. He concludes

---

[8] See the two chapters of Sternberg 1987 that center on character: chap. 9, 'Proleptic Portraits,' pp. 321–341, and chap. 10, 'Going from Surface to Depth,' pp. 342–364.
[9] Alter 1981, 127.
[10] Alter 1981, 126, 129.

that, even though 'there is little doubt that in classical writers characters were presented as types,'[11]

> it does seem plausible that [ancient] reading conventions that demanded that the reader infer character indirectly from words, deeds, and relationships could allow even for the typical character to fluctuate between type and individuality. If so, then it would seem wise to understand characterization, for any biblical text at least, on a continuum. This would imply for narratives like the gospels that the focus should be on the degree of characterization rather than on characterization as primarily typical.[12]

The degree of characterization – that is, the extent to which characters stand out as mere functional agents as opposed to individual personalities – indeed varies at different points of each gospel narrative. Jesus' disciples in Mark are a typical example. At one end of the continuum, they are, quite evidently, 'agents about whom nothing is known except what is necessary for the plot.'[13] This is true of the two anonymous disciples whom Jesus sends to fetch him a colt for his triumphal entry into Jerusalem (Mark 11:1–7), and the two he sends to make preparations for the Passover meal (14:12–16). In each case, the two disciples are needed for the miraculous to occur and for no other reason. At the other end of the continuum, there are figures like the one particular disciple whose portrait probably comes closest of all in the gospels to deserving the attribute 'human,' namely Peter.

'Peter the Image of Man'

Through what specific means is this human portrait achieved? What exactly is it about the character Peter that invites the reader to view him as an individual personality? Let us begin with the following *distance factors* in Peter's characterization, as listed by Thomas Boomershine in a groundbreaking study on Mark's narrative: Peter is the first disciple to be named, to be called and to accept the call; he is mentioned separately in expressions like 'Simon and his companions' (Σίμων καὶ οἱ μετ' αὐτοῦ, 1:36), or 'his disciples and Peter' (16:7); in the official calling

---

[11] Burnett 1994, 6.
[12] Burnett 1994, 15; cf. 1, 19. Burnett refers at this point to Adele Berlin (1983, 32), who similarly suggests that we should think of degrees of characterization as points on a continuum of agent to type to character.
[13] Cf. Berlin 1983, 32.

of the twelve (3:13–19), he is at the head of the list and is the only one given an individual surname; together with James and John, who are given a joint surname (and sometimes together with his brother Andrew), Peter forms part of 'the inner circle' of the twelve whose members are at times allowed to experience more than the other disciples (cf. 5:37; 8:2; 13:3; 14:33); he is the only disciple whose individual inner thoughts and emotions are described; together with John he is the only disciple whose words are ever reported (Peter five times: 8:29; 8:32; 9:5; 10:28; 11:21; John once: 9:38).[14]

Significantly, one of Peter's narrative functions is to express 'a human response that is totally believable.'[15] He represents a typical everyman who reacts in a way the reader might think anyone would. When Jesus tells his disciples about his suffering, Peter refuses to accept it (8:32); on the mountain of Jesus' transfiguration he does not know what to say, so he desperately tries to make the blissful moment last (9:5); upon hearing that it is necessary to leave everything for the kingdom, he quickly remarks, 'Well, that is exactly what we have done, haven't we?' (10:28); when he sees that the fig-tree Jesus cursed has withered, he is openly astounded (11:21); when Jesus suggests that all his disciples will desert and deny him, Peter is determined to correct him: 'all except me' (14:29); finally, having denied Jesus after all, Peter bursts into tears (14:72).

Especially in the story of denial, Peter's character is treated in an intimate way, so that 'this scene encourages the reader to take an interest in the character or "personality" of Peter himself.'[16] Here as elsewhere in Mark's narrative, Peter is driven by what constitutes his *primary dramatic need*: *the need to be a good disciple*. More than anything else, it is actions generated by this very need that lay the basis for the readers' construction of Peter's character.

At first, it really seems as if things will turn out the way Peter said they would: in 14:50, we are told that 'all of them deserted him and fled;' in 14:54, we learn that Peter indeed was an exception and followed on into the courtyard of the high priest after Jesus' arrest. The narrator may be playing a game with the readers' expectations at this point, delaying a little the information concerning Peter's part in the story.

[14] Boomershine 1974, 136–139.
[15] Boomershine 1974, 137.
[16] Burnett 1994, 22; see Boomershine 1974, 190; Tannehill 1977, 151; Rhoads and Michie 1982, 129.

Remembering the dialogue between Peter and Jesus in 14:29–31, readers are likely to ask 'How about Peter?' when they learn that all the disciples fled. Instead of immediately telling them about Peter, however, the narrator reveals that *somebody else* tried to follow Jesus: a young man wearing nothing but a linen cloth (14:51–52). Only after the arresting party's mission is complete and Jesus has been taken to the high priest (14:53) does the narrator point out that Peter indeed has followed along, at a distance, and is now in the courtyard. As Peter takes his place among the guards, warming himself in the firelight, the narrator leaves him for a moment and goes on to report the night trial of Jesus.[17]

With verse 14:66, the scene returns to *Peter's* trial. Peter is 'below' (κάτω) in the courtyard, while Jesus is 'above' in the high priest's house. A servant girl enters, and the readers are granted a view of Peter *from inside the narrative*: 'When *she saw* Peter warming himself, she stared at him and said . . . ' (14:67). The distance has grown shorter. Suspense starts to grow gradually, beginning from the words the girl 'stared (ἐμβλέψασα) at Peter.' Following 'The Rule of Three' that is typical of folktale narration as well as of Mark, suspicion and denial occur three times. First the servant-girl says to Peter: 'You also were with Jesus, the man from Nazareth.' Peter denies this and escapes to the forecourt. There the girl sees him again and reports her notion to others: the threat increases.[18] 'The bystanders' (οἱ παρεστῶτες) take up the servant-girl's notion and start questioning Peter: the suspicion is spreading among those around him. A steadily escalating suspense is felt by the audience in relation to Peter: on the one hand, we hold our breath to see whether he will be caught for following Jesus; on the other hand, we are waiting to see if he will keep the promise he made to Jesus (14:31), or if it is rather Jesus' prophecy (14:30) that will come true.

At first, Peter does not deny Jesus directly; what he denies is 'knowing or understanding what the servant-girl is talking about' (οὔτε οἶδα οὔτε ἐπίσταμαι σὺ τί λέγεις, 14:68). When asked for a second time – this time Peter's words are reported indirectly – he denies 'being one

---

[17] According to Boomershine, it is significant that the word used for fire here is not τὸ πῦρ but τὸ φῶς. This makes the scene metaphorical: by following Jesus, Peter has ventured to *come into light*, running the risk of being identified and being caught. That such a risk existed becomes clear not only from the servant-girl's questions to Peter a few lines later, but also from the report that the young man who tried to follow Jesus actually got caught; his person, too, was unveiled, so that he had to flee naked, in a shameful way.
[18] Boomershine 1974, 186.

of them' (καὶ ἡ παιδίσκη ἰδοῦσα αὐτὸν ἤρξατο πάλιν λέγειν τοῖς παρεστῶσιν ὅτι οὗτος ἐξ αὐτῶν ἐστιν. ὁ δὲ πάλιν ἠρνεῖτο, 14:69–70). Being asked the same thing three times is, finally, too much: Peter explicitly denies knowing Jesus.[19] The suspense is finally resolved, and the second cockcrow follows (14:72). Immediately after that – for the first time in the scene, so that the effect comes as if by a rapid zoom – we are granted *Peter's point of view* by means of a remembrance: 'Then *Peter remembered that Jesus had said to him,* "Before the cock crows twice, you will deny me three times."' The prophetic words uttered by Jesus in verse 14:30 are repeated almost verbatim as they echo in Peter's head. Only after we have first been invited to see things from Peter's position do we get the report of his reaction: καὶ ἐπιβαλὼν ἔκλαιεν . . ., 'And he broke down and wept.' This is where the scene ends, where we leave Peter – forever, for not once shall we meet him again in the gospel – weeping in the courtyard of the high priest. Who would not feel sympathy for the poor man? Who is the reader who would not greet with great relief and welcome the extra mention by the young man at the grave, 'the disciples *and Peter*' (16:7), letting us know that for Peter, too, it will be all right? As Auerbach puts it,

> Without any effort on [the author's] part, as it were, and purely through the inner movement of what he relates, the story becomes visually concrete. And the story speaks to everybody; everybody is urged to take sides for or against it . . . The incident [of Peter's denial], entirely realistic both in regard to locale and dramatis personae . . . is replete with problem and tragedy. Peter is no mere accessory figure serving as illustratio . . . He is the image of man in the highest and deepest and most tragic sense.[20]

How an Agent Becomes a Person

'*Without any effort on the author's part, as it were . . .* '. Auerbach's words underline the random nature of Peter's personhood, pointing out that the first disciple's personal tragedy sprouts up as an incidental by-product of the more prominent, cosmic tragedy of Jesus' passion. Once the seed of character is sown, it starts to grow, the sower does not know how. This process is further described by Frank Kermode in a study on the

[19] Cf. Boomershine 1974, 187; Tannehill 1977, 151.
[20] Auerbach 1953 (1946), 47–48, 41.

tradition history of the passion narrative as 'a fabula, progressively interpreted.'[21]

Kermode points out how the narrative grows and becomes more detailed due to interpretative retelling: new details require additional interpretation which, in turn, calls for more narrative, and so on: Achilles keeps chasing the tortoise. During this process, characters who could be conceived of as mere agents, plot functions, or actantial roles (such as 'betrayer' and 'deserter,' or 'helper' and 'opponent') on the atomistic level, gradually turn into more and more complex figures with genuine personality traits.[22] As a case in point, Kermode examines the development of the figure of Judas.[23]

In the beginning, betrayal is a motif included in the passion tradition. In 1 Corinthians 11:23 Paul recounts: 'the Lord Jesus *on the night when he was betrayed* took a loaf of bread . . .' However, once Jesus' passion is presented in the gospels as a story, the character of the betrayer becomes necessary for performing the act of betrayal. So in Mark, the first gospel, 'betrayal' becomes 'Judas, one of the twelve,' who is also introduced at the scene of the Passover meal.[24] But why should Judas want to betray Jesus? The answer is, for money, and so an episode in which Judas visits the chief priests is added to the story. Because the hero of the story – Jesus – is omniscient, it is necessary that he knows he is to be betrayed, and by whom. This, too, calls for a new narrative, namely a prophecy by Jesus to his disciples during the meal: 'one of you will betray me, one who is . . . dipping bread into the bowl with me' (Mark 14:17, 20). Like many features of the Passion narrative, this line is constructed on the basis of an Old Testament passage. In this particular case, the passage comes from the book of Psalms: 'Even my bosom friend in whom I trusted, who ate of my bread, has lifted the heel against me' (Ps. 41:9). Finally, on the Mount of Olives, Judas leads the arresting party to Jesus.

---

[21] Kermode 1979, 81.

[22] When mentioning plot functions of the *fabula* and their actantial roles, Kermode is referring to Vladimir Propp's classic *Morphology of the Folktale* (1928, Engl. trans. 1958), and the equally well-known actantial model presented by A. J. Greimas (1966).

[23] See chap. IV, 'Necessities of Upspringing,' of Kermode 1979 (pp. 75–99).

[24] Following Jeremias 1966, 96, Kermode (1979, 84) presumes that, at an earlier stage, in a short traditional passion account, Judas had no part in the scene of the Last Supper. This is supported by the fact that in the scene of the arrest, Mark, Matthew and Luke all mention Judas in such a way as to make him seem like someone the reader has not heard of before. Mark and Matthew report that 'Judas, one of the twelve' ('Ιούδας εἷς τῶν δώδεκα) 'arrived' (Mark 14:43, Matt 26:47); Luke speaks of 'the one called Judas, one of the twelve' (ὁ λεγόμενος 'Ιούδας εἷς τῶν δώδεκα, Luke 22:47).

The act of betrayal crystallizes in the famous 'inversion of the holy kiss that would have followed the sacred meal.'[25]

At this point, we have come to know Judas as he is presented in the gospel of Mark. This is not very much yet – but certainly 'enough to ensure that there will be more.'[26] Matthew takes over, supplementing Mark's short report of Judas' visit to the chief priests (Mark 14:10–11) with an account of a dialogue: 'How much?' – 'Thirty pieces of silver' (26:14–16). Why thirty? Because in Zechariah 11:12–13 the Lord refers to thirty shekels of silver as 'this lordly price at which I was valued by them.' 'Throw it into the treasury,' says the Lord to Zechariah; later on, Judas goes and does likewise. What happens to the money then? 'They (the chief priests) used it to buy the potter's field as a place to bury foreigners' (Matt. 27:7). Why? Because 'then was fulfilled what had been spoken through the prophet Jeremiah' (Matt. 27:9).

While Mark's Judas remains a simple agent, Matthew starts to give him what might well be considered personal features. Whereas Mark simply makes all the disciples respond 'Surely, not I?' to Jesus' prophecy of his betrayal, Matthew gives an extra focus to the question by having Judas alone ask it. Moreover, it is Judas alone who gets an answer: 'You have said so.' After the necessary act of betrayal is performed in Gethsemane, Mark does not again mention Judas. Matthew, contrary-wise, follows the poor man to the end. After everything is over, Matthew's Judas shows more than emotion: he repents (Matt. 27:3). Moreover, throwing down the money in the temple looks very much like a genuine act of despair.

As to what ultimately happens to Judas, different versions of the story give different answers, each of which presents the character of Judas in a slightly different light. In Matthew, he commits suicide. Because Matthew has told us earlier that Judas repented, Judas' decision looks like an effort to make amends for what he has done. This would allow us to think there was still a drop of dignity and nobility in his character. In Luke's version (preserved in Acts 1), Judas makes use of the money he gained. Evidently, Luke's Judas is all too obdurate ever to repent. God's curse falls upon him, however, as he 'falling headlong . . . burst(s) open and all his bowels gush . . . out' (v. 18). Still another tradition, preserved by Papias, says that 'Judas swelled up to such a size

---

[25] Kermode 1979, 86.
[26] Kermode 1979, 86.

that a place where a wagon could pass was too narrow for him,' which 'makes his death resemble those traditionally reserved for tyrants and very wicked men.'[27]

Both Luke and John report the exact moment when Judas the man, a greedy thief who stole from the common purse of the disciples (John 12:6), turns into Judas the betrayer occupied by Satan (Luke 22:3; John 13:27) – an intriguing case of a character becoming possessed by his narrative role, as Kermode points out.[28] The famous Johannine supper scene makes a lot out of this diabolical metamorphosis. The moment when Jesus dips a piece of bread in the dish and gives it to Judas is pregnant with meaning. In one narrative event, no less than three significant things take place: the prophecy in Psalm 41:10, 'who ate of my bread, has lifted the heel against me,' comes true; 'the beloved disciple' learns who the betrayer is; and Satan enters into Judas (13:26–27). Judas' fate, decided in advance by God (17:12) and put into effect by the devil (13:2), is (quite literally) in Jesus' hands. Eventually, it is Jesus who orders Judas to do what he is going to do. Judas obeys more or less automatically: 'So, after receiving the piece of bread, he immediately went out' (13:30). The overall effect produced by the scene is sombre – and even more so, because Judas' departure is followed by the extremely dramatic words ἦν δὲ νύξ, 'and it was night.'

Later, outside the four canonical gospels, Judas' character came to have an entire life of its own. In medieval legends, his bad habits were thought to be due to his harsh domestic conditions, for example. To quote Kermode, the whole matter is

> . . . really quite simple. Of an agent there is nothing to be said except that he performs a function: Betrayal, Judgment. When the agent becomes a kind of person, all is changed. It takes very little to make a character: a few indications of idiosyncrasy, of deviation from type, are enough, for our practised eyes will make up the larger patterns of which such indications can be read as parts.[29]

A Subject in Bud

In all their reticence and minimalism, biblical narratives make a very representative case of how little it takes for 'a kind of person' to emerge.

[27] Kermode 1979, 87.
[28] Kermode 1979, 85.
[29] Kermode 1979, 98.

Occasionally, these small seeds of individuality may grow unchallenged, as in Judas' case. At other times, however, they seem to have fallen on rocky ground and become scorched by the sun. Here the reception history of some minor characters in Mark provides us with a good example.

In a typical Markan healing story, the functions of the roles given to characters follow a regular pattern. Recently, David Rhoads has examined eleven healing stories as representative of a 'healing type scene "A Suppliant with Faith"' in Mark.[30]

The term 'type scene' originates with Robert Alter. It is a scene with certain characters and interactions that is repeated throughout the narrative. It sets up a convention, thus providing familiar patterns of expectation for the reader. Yet within the framework of 'the basic pattern that remains the same,' the details, forms and features of the type scene vary and introduce new elements to the story.[31]

Evidently, there is a pattern that repeats itself in the episodes: Rhoads is able to list up to twelve different elements that comprise the type scene of the 'Suppliant with Faith.'[32] In the particular case of the Syrophoenician woman, he is also able to recognize several points of contact with Mark's overall rhetorical/stylistic techniques, plotting, characterization, settings, standards of judgment, and so on. Furthermore, on the level of Mark's theology the topical role of *faith* ties all the different episodes together.[33]

Significantly, however, some figures who perform a similar role in their respective 'healing type scenes' receive a greater amount of *narrative subjectivity* than others. In other words, the narrative allows them more power to speak, act and perceive.[34] To illustrate this, I will consider two particular 'suppliants with faith,' namely, the paralytic whom Jesus heals

---

[30] The eleven stories are: Simon's mother-in-law (1:29–31); the leper (1:40); the paralytic (2:1–12); the man with the withered hand (3:1–6); Jairus' daughter (5:21; 35–43); the woman with the hemorrhage (5:25–34); the Syrophoenecian woman (7:24–30); a deaf and mute man (7:31–37); the blind man at Bethsaida (8:21–26); the father who brings a boy with an unclean spirit (9:14–29); Bartimaeus (10:46–52) (Rhoads 1994, 349).

[31] Cf. Alter 1981, 47–61.

[32] For structural and functional similarities between the stories – 'the basic pattern that remains the same' – see also Funk 1978.

[33] See Marshall 1989.

[34] Here I owe my choice of focus to Mieke Bal who, since the late 1980s, has been putting extensive effort into developing tools for the analysis of narrative subjectivity (for a synthesis, see e.g. chap. 6, 'Narrative Subjectivity,' in Bal 1991). In a wider perspective, Bal's work is part of her attempt to capitalize the ideological-critical potential of narratology.

in Mark 2:1–12, and the woman with the hemorrhage in Mark 5:25–34.

In the story about the healing of the paralytic, it is Jesus' authority to forgive sins that is the point at issue. What Jesus is able to do to demonstrate that authority is decisive. An additional function of the story – given that it is seen both in its immediate context and as an integral part of the gospel as a whole – is to contribute to the developing dramatic conflict between Jesus and his opponents.[35] These two functions interpenetrate the narration and dictate how much stage time each character gets.

As might be expected, it is Jesus who dominates the scene. The narrative includes patterns of three: three reports of a perception of Jesus; three references to his words 'your sins are forgiven;' three references to his words 'stand up and take your mat and walk;' and three references to the διαλογίζεσθαι, 'questioning,' of the scribes against Jesus.[36] The person healed, the paralytic, is brought to the stage very much like a material object: 'a paralytic carried by four was brought to Jesus.' There is, to be sure, a short private encounter between the healer and the paralyzed man. It is notable that Jesus calls the paralytic τέχνον, 'son,' or 'child,' but, because no more information is given, the form of address tells us more about Jesus than about the one to whom he is speaking. Significantly, *not once do we hear the voice of the man Jesus cures, or see the events through his eyes.*

The situation is quite different in the story of Jesus and the hemorrhaging woman. In this case, the audience is given information about the healed person, and also given an opportunity to see things from her point of view. The woman's past is given a vivid description; she is 'a woman who had been suffering from hemorrhages for twelve years; she had endured much under many physicians, and had spent all

---

[35] Since Wrede 1904, Mark 2:1–12 has conventionally been taken as an 'apophthegmatic narrative,' consisting of a controversy apophthegm secondarily embedded into a miracle story (cf. Bultmann 1968 [1931], 14–16, 212–213). As such, the narrative opens a section of five controversy stories in Mark 2:1–3:6. In her dissertation *Markan Public Debate: Literary Technique, Concentric Structure, and Theology in Mark 2:1–3:6* (Dewey 1980; see esp. pp. 109–143), Joanna Dewey has convincingly demonstrated that the section has a chiastic, concentric structure. It both begins and concludes with a healing story. The two healing stories are of a very similar type, constructed in a parallel manner as shown by form, content and linguistic details. Furthermore, 'along with the chiastic structure . . . there exists also a linear development of [intensifying] hostility in Jesus' opponents' (Dewey 1985, 113; cf. Dewey 1980, 109, 116, 118).

[36] Cf. Dewey 1980, 72; Marshall 1989, 81.

that she had; and she was no better, but rather grew worse' (Mark 5:25–26). In the Greek text, no less than five participles are used to define the single word γυνή, 'woman.' Her fearfulness and great trust in Jesus are further shown to us by means of an inside view in verse 28: 'for she said, "If I but touch his clothes, I will be made well."' As she makes her move, two additional inside views report *a sudden sensual realization*. Both accounts begin with the words 'and immediately' (καὶ εὐθύς), which indicates the simultaneous occurrence of the two inner sensations with which the hasty, rushing movement of the story is abruptly brought to a complete halt: 'and immediately her hemorrhage stopped, and she felt in her body (ἔγνω τῷ σώματι) that she was healed of her illness' (v. 29); immediately aware (ἐπιγνοὺς ἐν ἑαυτῷ) that power had gone forth from him, Jesus turned about in the crowd and said, 'Who touched my clothes?' (v. 30). That indeed is the question: there are as many as five references to the woman's touch within just six verses (or six times in seven, if 'the whole truth,' πᾶσαν τὴν ἀλήθειαν, in verse 33 is counted): 'she touched his cloak' (v. 27); 'If I but touch his clothes' (v. 28); 'Who touched my clothes?' (v. 30); 'Who touched me?' (v. 31); 'who had done it' (v. 32). The references come from four different speakers: the narrator (v. 27), the woman (v. 28), Jesus (v. 30), and the disciples (v. 31).

In the very center is the secret interchange of power between the woman and Jesus. It is reported twice: once from the point of view of the woman, and once from the point of view of Jesus. The moment is surrounded by a five-piece montage of the outer action that caused the inner event to take place: the woman touching the cloak of Jesus. Narrative investment in one single motif is extensive. The disciples' comment in v. 31 takes care that no one in the audience misses the profoundly supernatural *intimacy* in the scene: pressed from everywhere by the crowd, Jesus still has felt the woman's touch – just as the woman in an immediate bodily sensation could feel the effect which that touch made.[37]

---

[37] Kermode (1979, 133) has noted that what is said in verse 30 to have gone out of Jesus at the moment the woman touched him is called δύναμις, 'power,' a word with sexual senses in the Greek language. The same can actually be said of the verb γινώσκω, 'to know,' in verse 29 (cf. e.g. Matt. 1:25; Luke 1:34 as well as Gen. 4:1, 17, 25; 19:8 in the LXX) and the verb ἅπτω, 'to touch,' (cf. e.g. 1 Cor. 7:1). S. L. Graham (1991, 149) considers the event a parasexual act. While I would not be prepared to concede that any sexual connotations in the narrative were intentional, the mere fact that they come so naturally to many interpreters nevertheless characterizes *the atmosphere of intimacy* so dominant in the episode.

The woman's inside thoughts and feelings are again in focus in verse 33: she comes 'in fear and trembling;'[38] she knows what has happened to her. She comes to Jesus – still on her own initiative[39] – and Jesus kindly calls her θυγάτηρ, 'my daughter,' thus 'using the language of family to welcome her back into the community.'[40]

Although the paralytic brought to Jesus and the hemorrhaging woman play a parallel role of a 'suppliant with faith' in a Markan type scene, the way they are presented as narrative subjects differs significantly. While the paralytic is closest to a mere agent performing a necessary plot function, the woman is pictured (albeit in quite a minimalistic way) as a character with personal feelings, sensations, relations and intentions.

Now, however minimal this increase in subjectivity may seem, it was enough for Matthew and Luke to take material action in their use of Mark's text. It is to the evident ideological implications of this editorial work that I will turn next.

The Lost Self

Significantly, both Matthew (9:18–26) and Luke (8:40–56) omit what in Mark's earlier account were the most crucial moments of the hemorrhaging woman's story. Missing in both the Matthean and the Lukan version are the zooming-in brought about by the inside view of the woman's mind just before she touches Jesus, and the double inner sensation Jesus and the woman secretly share at the moment of the touch. The story has changed to the extent that the representation of events and characters becomes almost exclusively focused on, in Auerbach's words, 'Christ's presence and mission.' Moreover, the later versions evidently move toward greater narrative monologism, that is, one authoritative voice and one authoritative angle of vision (shared by

---

[38] The numerous suggested explanations for the woman's fear (as listed in Theissen 1983 [1974], 134) include: breaking the purity regulations (Grundmann 1963, 115); shame at her disease (Klostermann 1950, 51); the feeling of having stolen power without authority (Holzmann 1901, 135); realizing that her action could be mistakenly understood as either a love charm or an attempt to get rid of her disease by passing it on. Notably, all these explanations add to the woman as a narrative subject by further describing why and how she reacted.

[39] Cf. Luke's version, in which the woman seems to have no other choice: 'When the woman saw that she could not remain hidden she came . . .' (Luke 8:47).

[40] Graham 1991, 150.

the narrator and Jesus), with no deviations. Should other points of view, such as the woman's perspective, seem to challenge this authority, they are excluded.[41]

The trouble is, of course, that *any* rendering of personal experience tends to be challenging, at least in the long run. Indeed, it has been suggested that forms which focus on personal experience will, as a rule, go hand in hand with a special *'culture of contestation,'* or *'contestatory symbolic forms,'* in folklore and premodern literature.[42] These are forms and signs that resist and challenge the ideological naturalization and mystification of the *status quo* in social relations. Whenever the individual with his or her experience is given a voice of his or her own, it tends to challenge any outwardly defined identity that is based upon affinity with the dominant, unified ideology (that is, the 'culture of affirmation.') This holds true especially for the experience of crisis (meaning a challenge to the dominant means of coping with whatever life brings), especially crises experienced by those belonging to the subordinate classes in society. In its minimalist form, this challenge consists of the mere representation of individual experience as separate, independent and disintegrated, in other words as the voice of the *Other.*[43]

A Marxist scholar would typically examine 'contestatory symbolic forms' in the light of the Marxist theory of class relations. Luigi Lombardi-Satriani writes:

> This contestation is on the part of the dominated against the dominators, on the part of the weak against the strong . . . One of the most obvious examples is the relationship between the sexes where women assume the obligatory role of inferior creatures with respect to males who are the creators and depositors of values . . .[44]

---

[41] Cf. Bal, who notes that the 'reception of such texts [whose subjectivity is problematic] shows a tendency towards naturalization, that is, a tendency to solve the problems and interpret the text in a unifying, reassuringly "natural" way.' The motive behind this is that the text's ideological impact should not become blurred. (Bal 1987, 21.)

[42] See Lombardi-Satriani 1975; Thompson 1990.

[43] Interestingly enough, modern fiction has also shown exactly the opposite trend. Many modern writers have, in various ways, tried to dissolve the concept of the individual character that they regard as a manifestation of bourgeois ideology. Likewise, for ideological reasons, many contemporary literary critics have been suspicious about a theory of character. As they see it, any such theory would require a stable, unified concept of the self; such a concept is, however, a mere fiction that serves the interests of the ideological *status quo.* (See Rimmon-Kenan 1983, 29–31; Bal 1987, 106.)

[44] Lombardi-Satriani 1975, 103.

The story of the hemorrhaging woman focuses on an individual woman in crisis. Furthermore, it represents a contesting anomaly in terms of how the gospels usually present Jesus. The norm is that Jesus is virtually omniscient. He can read people's thoughts at will. In the case of this particular woman, however, he is suddenly unable to do that. He is 'aware that power has gone forth from him,' but he cannot tell who the beneficiary is. In the Markan and Lukan versions, the anomaly is allowed to prevail. The disciples' (in Luke, Peter's) comment (Mark 5:31; cf. Luke 8:45) serves to soften the scandal: Jesus' abilities are still clearly of a supernatural kind. For Matthew, however, the deviation from the norm is too much: in his version the woman is caught in the act, so that Jesus' inner vision is never put to the test.

In Mark 7:24–30 (par Matt. 15:21–28), Jesus meets yet another woman, and in this case, too, the inner logic of the story makes him act 'unjesuslike' in terms of a more general norm. During the short encounter, the woman – a gentile, Syrophoenician by birth – persuades Jesus to heal her daughter, something that he initially did not regard as proper. Jesus thus shows an ability to back up and reconsider his views when faced with someone who can match wits with him in making parables. The story is 'a classic example from the ancient Near East of the clever request by an inferior to a superior in which there is an exchange of proverbial sayings.'[45] The Jesus it portrays, as opposed to the normative Jesus of the gospel kerygma, not only teaches with authority but also learns from other people.[46]

Again, the later the version, the smaller the scandal. In Mark's version, Jesus gives due credit to the woman, saying, 'For saying that (διὰ τοῦτον τὸν λόγον), you may go – the demon has left your daughter' (Mark 7:29). Matthew, however, does his best to safeguard Jesus' authority: it is not for the woman to outwit Jesus; nevertheless, *because of her faith* he grants her healing: 'Then Jesus answered her, "Woman, great is your faith! Let it be done for you as you wish"' (Matt. 15:28).

In neither of these two stories in Matthew does Matthew's Jesus ever lose control. Before Matthew, however, exactly the opposite was the case. The two women had the initiative, and Jesus had to adapt.

---

[45] Rhoads 1994, 358, referring to Fontaine 1979.

[46] As Graham (1991, 151) points out, nor is it very often that a woman's speech is recorded in the gospel. Another such occasion is in the story of John the Baptist's death – also an exceptional story for being the only one in the gospel which does not center on Jesus.

For Matthew in particular, 'silencing the other' seems to have developed into a policy with a fixed purpose. One representative feature of his way of compressing Markan miracle stories is the very *reduction in dialogues*. Apparently, in Matthew's view 'a Jesus who engages in conversation does not fit the picture of the miracle worker who acts with divine authority.'[47]

As noted by Norman Petersen, many redaction-critical studies seem to indicate that the 'literary peculiarities of Matthew's gospel' – the way Matthew differs from its literary predecessor Mark – 'make it look – and function – like a *manual of discipline* analogous to the *Qumran Community Rule* (1QS), and the Christian *Didache*.'[48] Such works are intended to provide a community with a solid, unchanging (*incontestable*), enduringly homogeneous social structure of knowledge, belief and living. This is what Matthew, too, is up to. It would, however, be rather unfair to condemn him as a petty propagandist for doing just that. After all, he is only exemplifying a more general line of development that took place when the Christian community became more stable and better adapted to the *status quo*.

As time goes by, radical colors fade (or initially monochrome radicalism begins to show more colors, depending on the way you look at it). At first, a re-evaluation of socio-economic relations appears to have been part of the *metanoia*, the rethinking of the values and ways of life, that the early Christian communities proclaimed. According to Luke's testimony,

> all who believed were together and had all things in common; they would sell their possessions and goods and distribute the proceeds to all, as any had need . . . Now the whole group of those who believed were of one heart and soul, and no one claimed private ownership of any possessions, but everything they owned was held in common . . . There was not a needy person among them, for as many as owned land or houses sold them and brought the proceeds of what was sold. They laid it at the apostles' feet, and it was distributed to each as any had need. (Acts 2:44–45; 4:32, 34–35.)

Luke's vision of the early Christian community is in perfect harmony with the command Jesus gives to the rich man in Mark 10:21 (par Matt. 19:16–30; Luke 18:18–30): 'go, sell what you own, and give

---

[47] Theissen 1983 (1974), 178.
[48] Petersen 1994, 140, with reference to Bornkamm 1963, Robinson 1965, and Stendahl 1968.

the money to the poor.' According to Paul, no line of division drawn between different groups of people by social or religious institutions is valid in the Christian body. In Christ, all men and women are equal: 'There is no longer Jew or Greek, there is no longer slave or free, there is no longer male and female; for all of you are one in Christ Jesus' (Gal. 3:28). Moreover, the coming eschatological rule of God would turn the present order upside down:

> Blessed are you who are poor, for yours is the kingdom of God. Blessed are you who are hungry now, for you will be filled. Blessed are you who weep now, for you will laugh . . . But woe to you who are rich, for you have received your consolation. Woe to you who are full now, for you will be hungry. Woe to you who are laughing now, for you will mourn and weep. (Luke 6:20–21, 24–25.)

That is, of course, about as 'contestatory' as it can get.

While proclaiming a new kind of order, the early Christian movement quite probably did (as would any social movement challenging aspects of the present order and proposing new ones) create what might be called 'emancipatory space' – room for those under domination to have a voice of their own. Correspondingly, in the early Christian folklore traditions (as represented, for example, by some of the miracle stories preserved in the gospels) aspects of a personal, uninstitutionalized encounter of people with Jesus remain in focus. This kind of focus (besides being more or less 'contestatory' in itself) turns out to be, time after time, an occasion for unreservedly 'contestatory' actions and morals.

Yet any revolution – a point in history at which social values and ways of living are truly open to question – lasts only for a limited time. Gradually, a new Christian order developed with a new kind of hegemony. Individual experience tends to suggest questions – to be 'contestatory' by nature – and where answers are to be proclaimed, open questions are not pertinent. In the subsequent retelling of the story, the hemorrhaging woman loses even that short moment of intimacy she initially shared with her healer, and the Syrophoenician woman's contest with Jesus (and triumph over him) is eventually turned into a humble affirmation of the rule of faith.[49]

---

[49] This line of development extends beyond the limits of the canon; as a rule, problematic biblical stories involving women subjects 'become less problematic, smoother, but also less interesting' in their later cultural uses (Bal 1987, 5).

*

In the gospels, characters are most often not yet quite complete. In the event of being read, some of them increase, while others decrease. Which way it will go depends on how each character relates to the ideology of each gospel and to the ideology of its readers. In this respect, biblical characters resemble living organisms that mutate in order to adapt to their environment. This makes all static, comprehensive and harmonious interpretations of these characters problematic. As is the case with real-life personalities, partial truths are the only ones available.

Nevertheless, new 'conclusive' interpretations of biblical characters are likely to be proposed in the future, too. Even if the evangelists did not succeed in making their narratives completely monologic, there will be sympathetic critics to help them in this task. Confident that 'the presence of inconsistencies in no way undermines the unity of a narrative but simply becomes one of the facets to be interpreted,'[50] sincere critics will search until they find a literary interpretation that successfully integrates any inconsistent features into a complete whole. The trouble is that this can hardly be deemed as *critical* praxis. Even if we did not mind accepting the ideology of the evangelists, accurate critical description alone would require that the ideological dissonance in the text be noticed.

As in narratives, so in criticism, the tendency towards unity and monologism is strong, because it is, ultimately, ideological. This is natural in biblical studies because 'the text that is considered is identical with that which believing communities identify as authoritative for their faith and practice.'[51] Furthermore, there may also be a deeper existential need in all of us to keep the world as one, conceivable and naturalized; perhaps Mieke Bal is right when she wonders whether 'the convention of unity, so powerful in our history of criticism, is seductive because of its potential to keep the disturbing uncertainty of the subject buried.'[52]

[50] Powell 1990, 92.
[51] Powell 1990, 88.
[52] Bal 1987, 21.

7

The Gospel as a Plot

Along with character and point of view, plot has traditionally been among the most central areas of interest in narrative poetics. Correspondingly, attention to the ways in which the plot unfolds in each of the four gospels has been a salient characteristic of 'new literary approaches' to the New Testament, and of narrative criticism in particular. 'Older,' mainline research on the gospels has largely neglected plot.[1]

Or has it? That depends (somewhat obviously) on the sense in which the word 'plot' is used. Within narrative theory, different people use it in different ways. Some regard it as an aspect of the *content*, the 'what' of narrative.[2] In this case, the plot is often assumed to follow some basic structure that may start with an *opening* and proceed from the setting of *controversy* towards a *conflict* and its *solution*.[3] Moreover, some scholars have tried to classify different variations of this or another basic structure as distinct *plot types*.[4]

On the other hand, plot can also be understood as *the formal dimension – the 'how' – of narrative*. This echoes the Russian formalists who made the famous distinction between *fabula* and *sjuzhet*. *Fabula* refers to the basic events (*motifs*) of a story in their natural, causal-temporal order, whereas *sjuzhet* means the arrangement of the events of the story in the actual narrative. *Sjuzhet* is usually translated into English as 'plot.'

Finally, plot can also be conceived of in a far more general sense as *'the global dynamic (goal-oriented and forward-moving) organization of narrative constituents which is responsible for the thematic interest (indeed,*

---

[1] Cf. Moore 1989, xxi.
[2] Thus e.g. Chatman 1978.
[3] One famous characterization of such a structure is *Freytag's pyramid*. Introduced in Freytag 1894 (1863), this diagram describes the structure of a tragedy.
[4] Aristotle, of course, was among the very first to do this. For modern typologies, see e.g. Crane 1952 and Friedman 1955.

the very intelligibility) of a narrative and for its emotional effect.[5] When understood this way, plot seems to

> cut across the *fabula/sjuzhet* distinction in that to speak of plot is to consider both story elements and their ordering. Plot could be thought of as the interpretive activity elicited by the distinction between the sjuzhet and fabula, the way we *use* one against the other. (. . .) [W]e can generally understand plot to be an aspect of *sjuzhet* in that it belongs to the narrative discourse, as its active shaping force, but that it makes sense (as indeed *sjuzhet* itself principally does make sense) as it is used to reflect on *fabula*, as our understanding of the story.[6]

This is to say that plot is given a middle position as interpretive activity that takes place *between* the 'what' and the 'how' of narrative. It is by virtue of plot that narrative is able to work as an hermeneutic instrument, a structure of sense-making, a tool in the explication of meaning. Notably, narrative then does not need to be understood exclusively in terms of material texts. Encompassing all signifying practices (to use Antony Easthope's term), it rather appears as 'one of the ways in which we speak, one of the large categories in which we think.'[7]

This means, among other things, that the plot of each gospel can be viewed, not only as a literary but also, simultaneously, as a theological feature, a textual manifestation of (and contribution to) an historical process of ideological meaning-making, characterized by interpretive interplay between the form of proclamation and the message proclaimed, the way the evangelists 'use one against the other.'

This is how I will consider plot in this chapter. Basically, I will be looking for ways to examine the contribution of narrative to early Christian ideology, and vice versa. Why is it that the four gospels are narratives, and why is it that they are just the kind of narrative that they are?

Why a Narrative Gospel?

First of all, not all written gospels we know of are narratives. There are also *sayings gospels*, such as the lost gospel 'Q' (if you believe in it) and the Gospel of Thomas that was discovered only recently in Coptic

---

[5] Prince 1987. Prince derives this definition from the work of Peter Brooks (1984) and Paul Ricoeur (1984). Perhaps he should also note Kermode 1967.
[6] Brooks 1984, 13.
[7] Brooks 1984, 323.

translation. Why is it that only narrative gospels survive in the New Testament canon?

Some scholars have seen the rivalry between the two literary forms, the narrative gospels and the sayings gospels, essentially as a rivalry between two different ideologies. According to these scholars, the written gospel narratives emerged to refute theological views and social practices typically promoted by the sayings gospels and the traditions that preceded them.

To give an example: in an essay, 'The Gospels as Narrative,' James M. Robinson suggests that the historical circumstances which boosted the emergence of the narrative gospels involved two things in particular, namely (1) a need felt by the so-called mainstream church to defend the unity of the earthly and the risen Jesus against gnosticizing interpretations of Christianity that called this unity into question; (2) an attempt, again by the established mainstream, to neutralize the social radicalism of the early Palestinian Jesus-traditions into something more moderate and socially affirmative.[8]

According to Robinson, a comparative study of sayings traditions from the early strata of Q up to later Gnostic texts suggests certain historical lines of development. At an early stage, these traditions focus on the earthly Jesus. He is considered an envoy of wisdom, a prophet who suffered a typical prophet's fate. After his death, his prophetic words are preserved and passed on by some of his followers. At later stages, the focus shifts to the resurrected Jesus, who becomes identified with the Divine Wisdom. Even in heaven, he continues to instruct his followers through early Christian prophets and charismatics. These will keep adding new sayings – words of the living Jesus – to the tradition.[9] Gradually, the teachings that were received directly from the resurrected Lord in heaven begin to assume the status of a higher truth, an ultimate revelation.

---

[8] Robinson 1986; for a recent, somewhat similar, yet not identical account of 'a war of gospel types,' see Crossan 1998, 36–38. Essentially, Robinson's theory is an extension of the original insight, presented in William Wrede's classic work *Das Messiasgeheimnis in den Evangelien* (1901), that the narrative gospels represent an attempt to solve a discontinuity between traditions about the earthly Jesus and post-Easter Christian experience (cf. Robinson 1970 and Robinson 1978).

[9] According to a number of scholars, the Sayings Gospel Q represents a significant turning-point in this respect: 'While the dissolution of the word of the historical Jesus into the word of the heavenly Jesus had not yet occurred in Q, the center of gravity had shifted, so that Q was moving in the direction of a collection of "sayings of the living Jesus" such as the gospel of Thomas.' (Boring 1982, 182.)

From the mainstream point of view, on the other hand, there had to be a continuity between the earthly Jesus and the resurrected Lord. Should there have been a need to give special emphasis to either end of the continuum, it had better have been on the historical, this-worldly side. This was because the mainstream claim of apostolicity and orthodoxy rested heavily upon traditions that concerned the earthly Jesus. 'The twelve' were appointed, instructed, and sent to work by him. Should the teachings of the resurrected Lord become superior to these traditions, traditional apostolic authority would be challenged.[10]

Moreover, the sayings traditions were typically radical; they propagated a *metanoia* that had great potential for social criticism. This was also something that the mainstream may have found problematic. In social and cultural terms, the sayings traditions and the narrative gospels show a very different profile. Sociological studies of the Sayings Gospel Q have adopted the term 'itinerant radicalism' to describe the life-style valued by the early Palestinian followers of Jesus.[11] This life-style involved renouncing home, family, possessions and shelter. Those attracted by it were mostly poor, rural and illiterate people, peasants and fisherfolk. The evangelists, on the other hand, represented the 'moderately educated, literate, sedentary, cosmopolitan, hellenized' side of Christianity.[12] From their point of view, radical asceticism and anti-

---

[10] Robinson 1986, 104. Cf. Räisänen 1990, 217–222; 250–258, where Räisänen discusses traces of conflicts between Mark's post-Easter point of view and *early* Q traditions that center on the *earthly* Jesus and on his legacy. As Räisänen points out, a number of passages that relate to the typically Markan secrecy theme correlate in a negative way with the bulk of the Q tradition, especially in its early layers. What Mark suggests was kept secret by the earthly Jesus, and what his disciples did not understand were things that were originally unknown in Q. Apparently, the Q community had a different christological understanding than Mark; it did not give Jesus' passion and resurrection as much emphasis as Mark did; and it observed the Mosaic Law. For Mark, this was a problem. So he writes a narrative – a true story of how it really was that the Christian gospel began – in which Jesus reveals his true Messianic nature in mighty works of wonder; speaks of his death and resurrection as a matter of utmost importance; and teaches freedom from the Law. All this, so Mark suggests, was an integral part of the message of the earthly Jesus. Yet he also implies – and here the typically Markan secrecy theme plays a key role – that this was not universally known. Jesus only told these things to his disciples, and not even the disciples understood them at first – which, and this would have been Mark's point, also makes it understandable why some early Palestinian followers of Jesus, like the Q community, could still entertain an equally defective understanding.

[11] The term 'Wanderradikalismus' was first introduced in Theissen 1973.

[12] Robinson 1986, 106.

social behavior had no future; a more bourgeois Christian practice was required.

In Mark, the first narrative gospel, the relative lack of sayings of Jesus is striking, and even more so because Mark uses the word 'teaching' as a technical term to describe Jesus' ministry.[13] Moreover, in the whole of Mark, the risen Lord does not say a single word. At a number of points of his narrative, Mark emphasizes that all authoritative teaching had already been given to the disciples by *the earthly Jesus*, although they would only understand it after Easter. In Mark 13, post-Easter prophecy is mentioned in a critical tone: Jesus expressly notes, '*I have already told you everything*' (προείρηκα ὑμῖν πάντα); whoever will later 'come in my name' and 'produce signs and omens' is *a false prophet* (13:6, 22).[14]

On the other hand, the radical edge of Jesus' teaching is not concealed in Mark. Jesus' followers are called to 'deny themselves, take up their cross' and 'lose their life for the sake of the gospel' (8:34–35). As regards the prevailing social order and the powers that be, Mark is quite pessimistic. At times, it seems as if the authorities portrayed in the gospel were evil simply because they were authorities; a good Christian is portrayed as their complete opposite (10:42–45).

Nevertheless, with his recourse to narrative, Mark made a significant contribution to the future social adaptation of Christianity. Thanks to him, the radical ethos of the early Jesus movement became a feature *of the written gospel's fixed story-world*.[15] From this time on, this ethos could be romanticized, exalted, turned into a subject of nostalgia.

This is what many scholars think takes place in Luke's gospel.[16] Unlike Mark, Luke welcomes the sayings traditions from Q into his own narrative. At the same time, however, he *historicizes* the radicalism of

[13] Bultmann 1968 (1931), 342; Schweizer 1985, 45.

[14] Robinson 1986, 108.

[15] Mark's significance as the watershed which turned the living, immediate presence of Jesus in oral traditions into a distant, objectifiable *textual* Jesus is subjected to a full-length study in Kelber 1983.

[16] It has been a recent trend in scholarship to assume that, when composing his gospel, Luke had the establishment on his mind: the Roman officials, the well-off, the rich. Some say he wished to contribute to a peaceful coexistence between Christianity and the Roman empire (the original, classic version of this thesis was proposed by Hans Conzelmann [1957, Engl. trans. 1982]; later variations of the same theme include Walaskay 1983, Giblin 1985 and Esler 1987); others think he sought to interpret the original social radicalism of the Christian message anew for the rich and respectable (Schottroff and Stegemann 1986 [1978], Seccombe 1982).

these traditions by locating them in a golden age in the past. According to him, not only are these traditions to be traced back to the historical Jesus, but their message also properly concerns *the limited time of Jesus' earthly ministry*, as distinct from the (present) *time of the church* (see e.g. Luke 22:35–36).[17] As a result, the sayings traditions survive in Luke, but only as exhibits in a museum, where they might inspire but not disturb any current Christian practices. By programmatically separating the gospel's narrative world from the present 'time of the Church,' he succeeds in neutralizing what once was a radical challenge into a beautiful piece of memorabilia.

A Narrative Kenosis

Robinson's answer to the question 'Why are the gospels narratives?' is mainly historical and sociological: what he is saying is that particular ideological interests typical of particular historical circumstances called for the use of narrative. However, we might also put that same question more strictly in terms of narrativity and textuality. Starting from the gospels themselves, we would then ask how exactly are their observable theological or ideological objectives brought to narrative discourse.

As an example of this type of approach, we might refer to Paul Ricoeur's essay of 1990, 'Interpretative Narrative.' Like Robinson, Ricoeur suggests that the canonical gospels affirm the identity of the Christ of faith and the Jesus of history in a way that is possible only by means of a narrative. However, unlike Robinson, Ricoeur is not interested mainly in the history behind the text as an explanation of its present form, but rather in the narrative strategy that turns the kerygma into a plot; how does narrative design take on the task of ideological interpretation and, on the other hand, how does ideological interpretation assume the narrative mode?

Like a number of New Testament scholars, Ricoeur traces the initial narrativization of the kerygma back to the early, simple formulas such as 1 Corinthians 15:3–8 which states 'that Christ died for our sins in

---

[17] Here I am taking my lead from Hans Conzelmann's classic thesis, as presented in Conzelmann 1982 (1957). According to him, the theology of the Luke–Acts is based on a tripartite salvation-historical model: first, there was *the time of Israel* that lasted until Jesus; then there was *the time of Jesus' earthly ministry*, '*the middle of time*,' as Conzelmann called it; lastly, there was, and still is, *the time of the church,* which will continue until the Lord's return.

accordance with the scriptures, that he was buried, that he was raised on the third day in accordance with the scriptures, and that he appeared to Cephas, then to the twelve.' For Ricoeur, this passage contains a minimum, a *sine qua non* of narrativization that (as Helmut Koester once aptly put it) sets the pattern for gospel literature.[18]

This means that the events of Jesus' passion and resurrection become the gospel's natural *terminus*, the goal toward which the narrative as a whole is tending. Only after reaching that goal, and having made sense of it, can the narrative end. In this sense, Martin Kähler's famous definition of the gospel as a passion narrative preceded by a long introduction would seem to be quite apt.

The way the gospels make sense of Jesus' passion results in a particular narrative configuration. First, there is the *plot of action* that reproduces the chain of events which led to Jesus' death. Basically, this involves contingent human actions such as treason, denial, abandonment and flight. Second, the narrative will confront this human contingency with the inevitability of the divine plan: 'it was necessary that the Messiah should suffer these things and then enter into his glory' (Luke 24:26).[19] In other words, the plot of action will be supplemented by another, *hermeneutic plot* that aims at *discovery*. The narrative strives to show that the very same line of action that, at first glance, seems to disprove Jesus' Messianic claim, actually confirms it.

This means that, basically, a gospel narrative comprises classic elements. First, it involves a great *peripeteia*. Destined to glory, the supreme agent of God's rule and self-revelation will come to the world – only to become rejected and suffer a painful and humiliating death on the cross. Second, as a hermeneutic narrative, a gospel is all about the *recognition* of Christ Jesus for who he truly is. The characters in the story, and the audience who hears the story, are expected to gain a correct understanding of who Jesus is and what his words and deeds stand for.[20]

In theological terms, then, what takes place here is *a dramatized kenosis*: the sovereignty of the Messiah becomes muddled, questioned, disguised or concealed when Jesus 'humbles himself and becomes

---

[18] Ricoeur 1990, 240; Koester 1971, 161.

[19] Ricoeur 1990, 238–239. At this point, Ricoeur is drawing upon what Robert Alter has pointed out earlier concerning narratives of the Hebrew Bible (Alter 1981, 33, 189).

[20] Suffering, peripeteia and recognition (anagnorisis) are the elements which Aristotle, in his *Poetics*, considered the most certain to produce a tragic effect.

obedient to the point of death – even death on a cross' (cf. Phil. 2:8). The very same Christ whose glory is made transparent to the reader in miraculous signs and powerful teaching becomes momentarily opaque and *unrecognizable.*

Unlike Philippians 2, the dramatized (or narrated) kenosis does not take place in the event of incarnation. Hans Conzelmann was certainly right when he wrote in reference to Philippians 2:6–11: 'No gospel could be written in the light of this christology.'[21] At the beginning of each gospel, Jesus enters the world (or, as in Mark, begins his career, anointed by the Spirit) full, not empty, of God's power. This opening is followed by reports of signs, wonders, fulfilled prophesies and authoritative teaching which confirm that we are witnessing an epiphany. These are essential, because the discharge of Jesus' power will be displayed, not as a momentary (or timeless) mythical event, but in the framework of a historical narrative about the career of the earthly Jesus.[22] In order to be exhausted in the story, the figure of Jesus must be empowered first.

In its most rudimentary form, the configuration that results can be seen in Mark's gospel. Miracle stories abound in the first half. Initiated by Jesus' miracles, the motifs of wonder and acclamation then come to structure the gospel as a whole. Contrasted with Jesus' passion, they push the story towards the moment of peripeteia: 'He saved others; he cannot save himself' (Mark 15:31). Contrasted with the motif of secrecy, they push the story towards recognition; it is in reaction to miracles that the question of Jesus' identity becomes acute. Upon exorcism, the demons recognize him (1:24, 34; 3:11). After the stilling of the storm, the disciples ask in awe, 'Who is this?' (4:41). In his hometown, people wonder about his deeds of power, saying, 'Is this not the carpenter, the son of Mary?' (6:3). The miracle-maker's reputation entices different popular views of who he might be (6:14–15). These are later set in contrast with what his followers ought to think about him (8:27). So it goes on until, finally, witnessing the

---

[21] Conzelmann 1969 (1968), 80.

[22] Notably, the mere kenosis myth – or any myth, for that matter – *as such* would not make much of a story. In order for a genuine story to emerge, the myth has to be reworked, reverted and transformed – plotted – so that Jesus' surrender of glory and acceptance of passion can be pictured not only as a single, timeless event, but also as a dynamic action involving elements of complication (Cf. Kermode 1967, 18). Eventually, the result will be something quite like the present narrative gospels.

wondrous events accompanying Jesus' death, the Roman centurion affirms the authority that was given to Jesus from heaven when he first began his career: 'This man was God's Son (15:39; cf. 1:11)!' The circle has become complete.[23]

Thus, what the narrative does is to stage an epiphany, to veil it in the mystery of passion, to be recognized again as an epiphany by the reader. If we unwind this structure from its end, we will see how the theme of suffering extends over the entire gospel and indeed makes it a passion narrative with a long introduction. If, on the other hand, we focus first on the opening half of the story, we will notice how that, too, stretches out to saturate the whole, so that we might as well conclude that Mark has an *aretalogical composition*, 'based on the realization of motifs of secrecy and acclamation.'[24] In both cases, however, the pattern underneath is very much the same. It takes us first from extreme dignity to extreme humiliation and then back to the restitution of dignity, to be acknowledged despite the scandal of the cross.

Finally, in weaving this pattern, each narrative gospel becomes involved in a fundamental paradox. As both the epiphany and its eclipse are to be extremely effective, the one and the same narrative is supposed to hide and reveal, conceal and disclose. Obviously – as I have sought to show in the previous chapters of this book – to maintain the balance between these two dissonant goals is not an easy task. Moreover, it is the very management of this balance that decides whether (or better, to what extent) a particular gospel clings to narrative as its major hermeneutical mode, or whether (or how rapidly) it starts to develop towards more open and direct modes of theological interpretation. It is to this that I will turn next.

---

[23] Cf. Theissen 1983 (1974), 212–215.

[24] Theissen 1983 (1974), 215. This corresponds well to Robinson's earlier postulate, presented in Robinson 1970, that the key to understanding Mark's (and John's) composition is the notion that the evangelist correlates passion narrative with aretalogy. It is this correlation that makes Mark able to reconcile, in a single historical narrative, the traditions about the earthly Jesus with revelations of Jesus as resurrected. The key passage here is Mark 8 (and, in the case of John, John 16), where Jesus speaks to his disciples 'openly' (παρρησία): 'In the case of Mark and John, where the basic turning point is from an aretalogical public ministry to a kerygmatic crucifixion, the beginning of the period of higher revelation can be transplanted back from the resurrection appearances to the point at which the passion narrative is thematically initiated: Mark 8 and John 16' (p. 113).

Concealment and Disclosure

As hermeneutic, interpretive narratives, the gospels remind us of Jesus'
parables. On the one hand, they *reveal* a truth about divine intentions
that would otherwise remain hidden beyond the opaque surface of reality.
On the other hand, they *conceal* that truth in further riddles. Which of
these is given greater emphasis depends on each individual gospel
narrative.

Among the New Testament gospels it is Mark who allows most
emphasis on concealment. In the Markan Parable Theory, Mark has
Jesus declare that his parables are essentially a means of keeping the
secret of God's rule for insiders only.

Matthew and Luke make substantial alterations to the Markan text.
In Matthew 13:13, Matthew replaces the Greek conjunction ἵνα in
Mark's text with a new conjunction, ὅτι. This turns the key clause in
the Parable Theory, which in the Markan text would appear to be a
final clause ('*in order that* "they may indeed look, but not perceive,"
etc.'), into a causal one ('*because* "seeing they do not perceive," etc.').
Thus, in Matthew's version, the parables do not harden attitudes, but
rather represent an affliction God has assigned to those with hardened
hearts. It becomes even more difficult for them to receive what Jesus
has to say. What he says, however, he says openly to all people. In his
Sermon on the Mount, Matthew's Jesus presents an ethical program
that is fully comprehensible and is ready to be put into action: 'Everyone
then who hears these words of mine and acts on them will be like a wise
man who built his house on a rock' (Matt 7:24).

Luke, for his part, omits the concluding words of the Markan Parable
Theory concerning repentance and being forgiven (Luke 8:10).
Consequently, the emphasis is not on the hardening effect of Jesus'
words, but on the necessity to become an insider in order to understand
the secrets of God's kingdom. Significantly, the possibility to repent, to
be forgiven, and to become an insider, remains open to everyone.
Correspondingly, Luke's Jesus is fond of illustrative exemplary stories
in which the fixed character types present themselves as identifiable
prototypes of commendable Christian conduct: 'Go and do likewise'
(Luke 10:37).

In John, finally, Jesus is not really trying to hide anything. The trouble
is that it is impossible for a natural man or woman to understand what
he says. Spiritual talk remains a mystery for flesh and blood. In order to

conceive it, you must be born anew of the Spirit. This is demonstrated in scenes where people misunderstand Jesus, that is, take his parabolic words for their literal meaning.

A great parabolist, the Jesus of the gospels also turns out to be a parable himself. In a truly parabolic manner, his earthly appearance is simultaneously an epiphany and a secret which only some can understand. And in this respect, too, each individual gospel narrative adheres to its own distinctive policy of secrecy or openness.

In Mark, Jesus actively seeks to keep his Messianic identity a secret. His disciples may learn it, but even for them, the ultimate meaning of his fate remains a mystery. In Luke, Jesus is much less of a mystery person. Nevertheless, Luke accepts the idea presented in Mark that a final opening of the eyes will only take place after Jesus has actually risen from the dead. In Matthew and in John, Jesus makes an open epiphany (in John, this takes place to the extent that practically everything Jesus says or does is a testimony of himself). There is no question of secrecy, yet only few will recognize Jesus for who he truly is. In Matthew's story, this is because God has hardened the hearts of Israel, so that the good news will be passed on to the gentiles. In John, Jesus can be truly known, accepted and received only by the Spirit.

In the end, it is very much these adjustments to the basic plot of discovery that make each of the four gospels a different story. Moreover, in some gospels the plot determines the literary form of the work as a whole to a greater extent than in others. Thus, Mark and John are essentially *narrative christologies*, that is, stories about how the initially secret or incomprehensible Jesus reveals who he truly is. The narrative receives its rationale from a movement, or *desire*, towards what would be a conclusive, fully valid scene of recognition. What keeps the story going is the fact that this scene is continually postponed: people either fail to fully understand Jesus, or they misunderstand him. The composition of Matthew and Luke, on the other hand, while presupposing this same basic plot pattern, seems to draw more extensively on external formal influences. They present essentially a *life* of Jesus and a *manual* of Christian life, designed in line with prevailing literary conventions related to such purposes.[25]

---

[25] Here one might also refer to Norman Petersen who believes that, while none of the New Testament gospels properly fits any single known genre, Matthew and Luke–Acts are close enough to make generic comparisons fruitful. As to Mark and John, in turn, Petersen prefers to speak not of narratives which are reminiscent of a certain literary genre, but

The Limits of the Narrative Gospel

Finally, in three out of the four gospels, all's well that ends well. The narrative reaches its goal and closes with a final recognition scene, or an entire series of them. In Mark's gospel, however, this obviously predestined end of the story never comes. In what is widely considered the original ending of Mark, the narrative closes well before attaining what would seem to be its natural conclusion. There is no final scene of recognition where incomprehension ends and the meaning of Jesus' fate becomes truly known. There is rather a disquieting, anticlimactic silence: having been entrusted with the task of spreading the news of Jesus' resurrection, his women followers 'went out and fled from the tomb, for terror and amazement had seized them; and they said nothing to anyone, for they were afraid' (Mark 16:8).

Frank Kermode has made the fine point that Mark's open ending is a metonymy of the gospel's own, metonymic condition as a narrative.[26] Indeed, all narrative explanation is, of necessity, inconclusive. As a metonymic relation, '[t]he relation between fabula and sjuzhet, between event and its significant reworking, is one of suspicion and conjecture, a structure of indeterminacy which can offer only a framework of narrative possibilities rather than a clearly specifiable plot.'[27] As the afterlife of the gospels in the apocrypha, legends, and theological as well as literary interpretations suggests, no narrative truth about Jesus is either unambiguous or final.

We might thus say that, among the New Testament gospels, Mark is the one which most willingly submits to the inescapable limits of its own narrativity. This is also Kari Syreeni's point, when he describes Mark as a *metaphoric gospel* that abstains from open and direct proclamation and is content with merely 'whispering in the reader's

---

merely of narratives of a certain *plot type* – namely, 'concealment/recognition type' and 'disclosure/reception type,' respectively. In the 'concealment/recognition type' (Mark included), 'a divine being appears in human form to human beings and for a time conceals her or his identity' (Petersen 1994, 153). In the disclosure/reception type of narrative (such as John), the divine being in a human form does not conceal his or her identity, but openly discloses it. 'Whether, and with what consequences, the human beings will accept or reject what is disclosed to them,' is in focus (Petersen 1994, 155).

[26] Kermode 1979, esp. pp. 66–71.
[27] Brooks 1984, 275.

ear:' '*This story has to do with your life, too, hasn't it?*'[28] Compared with Mark, later gospels tend all the more towards a more open and direct rhetoric of proclamation. Luke, for one, moves towards an essentially *paradigmatic gospel* where 'a sensitive reader may have the feeling that [the narrative] has already been interpreted.'[29] In John – as well as in later Gnostic gospels – all secrets are openly revealed in Jesus' direct speech. At this point, as Syreeni points out, the death of the narrative gospel is already close at hand.[30] For the purposes of presenting authoritative Christian views plainly and clearly, one will need to resort to literary forms and practices that can claim to be something more than just suspicion and conjecture.

[28] Syreeni 1991, 52.
[29] Syreeni 1991, 52.
[30] Syreeni 1991, 54.

Part III

8

The Future of Narrative Criticism: A Paradigm Shift

Reconceiving Narrative Criticism

I began this treatise on narrative criticism by discussing David Rhoads' seminal article of 1982, 'Narrative Criticism and the Gospel of Mark.' Rhoads first summarized the basics of narrative criticism as a literary approach. This was at the time when narrative criticism was just about to come into its own.

It is appropriate, then, that I should now, in this concluding part of my work, consider another, more recent essay of Rhoads, entitled 'Narrative Criticism: Practices and Prospects' (1999). As the title suggests, Rhoads evaluates (once more) the present state and future possibilities of narrative criticism. After reflecting on various critiques of the method, he goes on to assess how narrative criticism continues to evolve and transform.

Intriguingly, 'Narrative Criticism: Practices and Prospects' combines two somewhat dissonant objectives. First, it persistently emphasizes *the specific identity of narrative criticism*. As distinct from all other approaches, it is said to focus on *the surface level of narrative*, to grant it *value* in its own right, and to use it as basis of imaginative reconstructions of how (original or subsequent) readers may have experienced the narrative's *impact*. Thus, a distinctively poetic interest continues to be one of its salient characteristics. In part, the future promise of the method lies in its openness to the development and application of new and better techniques *that advance this interest*.

Second, Rhoads accentuates the *openness and inclusiveness of narrative criticism in relation to other methods* old and new: comparative literary history, genre criticism, rhetorical criticism, 'orality criticism,' performance criticism, social-science criticism, ideological criticism. In furtherance of their goals, narrative critics will strive to be methodologically as comprehensive as possible, and they should ensure that the interpretations they suggest are responsible and ethical.

It would be difficult to object to any of Rhoads' hopes as such. What could be a better future for narrative criticism than to develop as an essentially open system in terms of advancing its own techniques and learning from others? What remains in question, however, is the nature of this wider interpretive framework in which those hopes might be realized.

Evidently, there is no return to the old historical-critical paradigm. The traditional exegetical methods of *Literarkritik*, form criticism and redaction criticism, simply did not account for the particularity of the gospels *as narratives*. In this respect, narrative critics had a clear case from early on. On the other hand, the traditional literary paradigm in which narrative criticism originated has turned out to be problematic as well. At worst, it is severely unconcerned with its own historicity as well as with the historicity of its subject of study, 'literature.' If this paradigm is not replaced with something new, the long-awaited incorporation of disciplines such as ideological criticism and cultural exegesis just may not take place.

Thus, I would like to propose that narrative criticism should assume yet one more future objective. Besides becoming technically more advanced and methodologically more inclusive – a better science of textual engineering as it were – it might also once more promote essentially hermeneutic reflection and reconsideration of the entire framework of biblical interpretation as a whole. This would involve a paradigm shift comparable to that which, in his original 1982 article, Rhoads envisioned would take place once gospel studies made the transition from historical to literary study. This time, however, the shift will have to be from literary study into something new. What this will be is not exactly clear yet.[1] If I may draw a parallel with the 'two shifts of perspective' once suggested by Rhoads (one a shift from fragmentation to wholeness and the unity of the narrative, the other from history to

---

[1] Within the guild of literary scholars, an explicit call for a paradigm shift has recently been voiced by a movement known as *cultural studies*. This movement rejects traditional, essentialist and exclusivist ideas of literature, canon and value, and seeks to focus on all types of everyday 'signifying practices' as textually specific cultural processes. See e.g. Easthope 1991 – a book properly titled *Literary into Cultural Studies*. For a broader introduction to cultural studies as a multidisciplinary movement, see Grossberg, Nelson and Treichler (eds) 1992.

fiction and textual autonomy), I would venture to suggest *two broadenings of view*, one of the 'vertical,' the other of the 'horizontal' type.[2]

'Vertically,' the new paradigm would dissolve the autonomy of textuality so as to account for the historical, social and cultural contingency of any linguistic (and especially, 'literary') expression. In contrast to the traditional notion of poetics that regarded 'literary' approaches and historical, sociological or cultural approaches as mutually exclusive, poetics as conceived in the framework of the new paradigm would inevitably be historical, social and cultural. Literary meaning and value would be *demythologized*, made a consistent part of variable historical reality.

'Horizontally' – and this is but a logical corollary of the initial 'vertical' stance – all historical (textual, material, social and cultural) dimensions of *the entire communicative act/interpretive situation* involving the author, the text and the reader should be in focus. The production, form and reception of texts are neither static nor fully autonomous categories. Every linguistic act, every artistic creation necessarily implies an event of reception, an encountering with 'the other.' Moreover, it is the readers who first decode the potentialities of the text into some actual effect, thus properly making the text, writing the text, speaking in the text as they read. Again, all this takes place in immanent history, amidst particular material, social and cultural conditions.

In biblical studies, all this is less of a novelty than it first might seem. For one thing, modern biblical criticism has, for its entire history, been about the *textual features, theology* and *history* of the biblical documents. Thus, the 'vertical' complexity of the subject matter is already implicit in current praxis. The question now is about establishing the right balance between the different aspects of study, so that no single dimension of the biblical text is either overemphasized or neglected.[3] We also need to become fully aware of the fact that none of the three fields involved is properly independent of the others. Even as 'literary' entities, textual features are essentially historical and ideological. As a (in itself diverse and polyphonic) set of social constructs, 'New Testament theology' is a textual fiction that makes sense of historical experience. History, finally, can only make sense as interpreted, and can only be

---

[2] Rhoads 1982, 412.
[3] Cf. Syreeni 1997, 112; Robbins 1996a, 14.

communicated in textual form (even if this form need not necessarily be that of ordinary language).

Second, the interpretive situation involving the horizons of the author and the reader, and the text as their meeting-point, has traditionally been within the scope of biblical *hermeneutics*. Thus, it is not surprising that, of all literary-theoretical models it is Seymour Chatman's model of narrative as communication that has become so well-received among biblical critics. Although exclusively textual, this model nevertheless perceives the text as a *relationship of mediation*. In terms of the implied author and the implied reader, it even seeks to account for the presence of ideological interpretation – an unavoidable third party in the two-pole act of narrative communication.

Not unexpectedly, then, current biblical scholarship has begun to show interest in *integrated approaches* that view different methods and points of view as partners in a common interpretive enterprise, each partner making a significant contribution that could not be achieved by other means, yet each also falling short of what they might achieve together.[4] Depending on the interpreter's own choice, this integration may be more or less radical. In any case, the different modes of investigation – typically, these are labeled as different types of 'criticism' – are expected to interrelate, although they may not necessarily be required to change in other respects. Poetics may remain 'literary' and 'text-intrinsic,' if it so pleases; its blind spots will then be observed, yet they will be compensated by means of other, complementary methods and points of view.

We should also be aware of the return of historical interest in some radically new forms. A truly promising cross-fertilization of social history, comparative studies in ancient Greco-Roman literature, and insights taken from theoretical movements such as 'cultural studies' and 'new historicism' is well under way in several units of the Society of Biblical Literature. This can, with good reason, be expected to pave the way for a new perception of poetics as an historically, socially and culturally conditioned encounter between textual products and their recipients.

Most concretely, the new paradigm is being hammered out in the context of certain individual syntheses that explicitly and systematically, yet often in a delightfully personal manner, seek to construct an entire new environment of interpretation for biblical studies. Below, I will

---

[4] See (in addition to Rhoads 1999), e.g. Tate 1997.

discuss two representative cases that I think deserve mention for their promise and insight. These are Kari Syreeni's *hermeneutic model of three worlds*, and Vernon Robbins' *model of socio-rhetorical criticism*. It is no coincidence that both of these models are based on a pragmatic combination of social-scientific and literary-critical approaches. Furthermore, each of them combines a system of multiple levels of analysis with a system of multiple foci that takes into account the situation 'behind' (issues related to origin and background), 'within' ('intrinsic' features) and 'before' the text (reception, interpretation, application).

A Cosmology of Interpretation: Kari Syreeni's Model of Three Worlds

In a series of articles published during the 1990s, Kari Syreeni has developed an interpretive framework which he calls a hermeneutic model of three worlds. In this model, Syreeni considers human reality in terms of three different spheres: the *text world* (aspects of intra- and intertextuality), the *symbolic world* (reality as a social construct; the level of ideology), and the *concrete, or real world* (everyday reality; the material conditions of existence). In order to attain a comprehensive view of what a text means and how, we need to consider all these three worlds as subjects of analysis and, to avoid misinterpretation, we must not confuse any of them with any other.

As Syreeni himself explains, his tripartite model is essentially a combination of two dualistic models, one sociological model that makes a distinction between an ideological 'superstructure' and a material 'substructure' of reality, and one that he calls a 'literary paradigm', or the 'linguistic and literary-critical standard distinction between text-world and real life.'[5] Later, he also made a connection between his model and the three worlds presented in the philosophy of Karl Popper,

[5] Syreeni 1990a, 128; Syreeni 1994, 523. On the sociological side, Syreeni is drawing on Berger's and Luckmann's classic work *The Social Construction of Reality: A Treatise in the Sociology of Knowledge* (1967). It is from there that he adopts the idea of the *symbolic universe* as a social construct, a person's or group's world view objectified in concrete life. The term symbolic *world*, in turn, refers to a similar type of entity objectified in a literary (or other) artefact. On the literary side, Syreeni's favorite quotation, in support of his claim that literary studies typically presuppose an essentially dualistic paradigm, comes from Scholes and Kellogg 1966, 82: 'Meaning, in a work of narrative art, is a function of the relationship between two worlds: the fictional world created by the author and the "real" world, the apprehendable universe' (see Syreeni 1990a, 128 n. 6; Syreeni 1994, 523 n. 4; Syreeni 1997, 106).

noting structural similarities but also significant differences between the two.[6]

In his recent work, Syreeni has supplanted this initially synchronic model with a diachronic view that enables him to consider all three parties involved in the event of communication (see Fig. 1). Thus, the *text* does not merely display the three dimensions of textuality, ideology

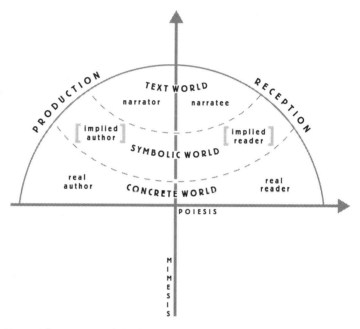

Fig. 1: The two axes and the three levels of analysis in a narrative text according to Kari Syreeni's 'model of three worlds.'

[6] According to Syreeni, his model differs from Popper's *emergent materialism* in three important respects. First, while Popper regards products of the human mind (objects in 'world 3') *in evolutionary terms* as monuments of human *understanding* (a typical world 3 entity is a *theory*), Syreeni's text-world entities are each *unique* cultural objects, 'expressions of life,' whose aesthetic properties and complexity of form play an important role. Second, in Popper's model, 'world 2' contains only *operations* of the mind but not their *immaterial products*; these belong to world three. In Syreeni's model, on the other hand, entities such as ideologies and world-views are properties of *the symbolic world*. Finally, for Popper, human reality is one and undivided: it is one natural reality, one human consciousness, and one cumulative cultural heritage that worlds 1, 2 and 3 describe. Syreeni's model, in turn, is a pluralist one, when it comes to the concepts of the text-world and the symbolic world: there are many texts and ideologies of several types. (Syreeni 1997, 115–119.)

120

and material existence. The *author* and the *reader* participate in the process of communication too, not only as the producer and receiver of textual features, but also as ideological actors and historical beings: one is transmitting an ideological construction of experienced reality and the other is interpreting it and putting it into practice in life. This process, as a whole, takes place along *an arch of communication* that starts from the physical reality, enters the arena of symbolic meaning in community, reaches the level of textuality, attains objectification in the text, returns to the world of ideas in the interpretation, and finally falls out of the symbolic sphere in the reader's responses as far as they alter the material universe. The text as *mimesis* is also shown to *represent reality* as social construction, while the text as *poiesis* appears as a structure of *reference and inference*.

Finally, Syreeni addresses the question of the interpretation and use of the text *outside its original communicative event* by distinguishing between *primary and secondary hermeneutics*. Secondary hermeneutics involves analysis of the original communicative situation. Strictly speaking, this has belonged to historical exegesis. The situation between the text and its interpreter as personally involved in the process of interpretation, in turn, is the issue of primary hermeneutics. In practice, this distinction is not absolute, but rather designates the end poles of a continuum: *Wirkungsgeschichte* and reception criticism, for example, are closer to primary hermeneutics than are the traditional exegetical methods, especially as far as the interpreter's own cultural and/or ecclesiastic tradition is concerned.

*

What, then, is the advantage of Syreeni's hermeneutic model of three worlds? Syreeni himself offers it not as an individual method of analysis, but as an 'interpretive framework,' 'a way of thinking' that invites certain typical questions – indeed, a new paradigm for biblical studies.[7] Any complexities inherent in the three-world scheme might well serve as an example of the kinds of questions a paradigm shift such as I have envisioned above would typically involve.

A combination of binary oppositions, Syreeni's model is by nature liable to deconstruction. One critical moment relates to the necessary

---

[7] On the other hand, he also suggests that the model may have methodological applications (Syreeni 1997, 119).

mutual interdependence of the three worlds, an issue that I have touched on above. Strictly speaking, this interdependence allows none of the three worlds to have an immediate, observable autonomy – which, ultimately, puts the entire model in danger of collapse. For 'reality' can only be spoken of *as a social construct in terms of language*, which means (in Derridean terms) that 'There is nothing outside the text.' Alternatively, to view the same thing the other way round, as material phenomena, textual features are beyond our limited access and can only be conceived of as ideological constructs so that 'There are no texts, only readings.'

On the other hand, however difficult in theory, a distinction between textuality, ideology, and physical reality may be useful in practice. There are (at least) two reasons for this.

The first reason is truly pragmatic: where no such distinction is made, confusion is almost certain to follow. To give an example: advertizing the benefits of narrative criticism, Mark Allan Powell proposes, as a result of narrative-critical analysis, that the strongly negative characterization of the Jewish leaders in Matthew's narrative is to be seen as a rhetorical device that the narrator uses in order to bring home an important theological lesson. According to Powell, the literary effect of Matthew's portrayal

> is to impress upon the reader that God, in Christ, has overcome evil, even though it succeeded at doing its worst. If Matthew softened his characterization of the leaders, made them less evil than they appear, the force with which this point is made would be weakened.[8]

Consequently, 'the religious leaders in Matthew's narrative do not 'stand for' any real people in the world *outside the story*, but are constructs of the implied author designed to fulfil a particular role *in the story*.' The fact that Matthew's gospel has aroused hostility towards Jewish religious leaders, and towards the Jews in general, is based on a misreading which 'represents a gross example of the referential fallacy and completely misses the point of the story.' Luckily, says Powell, 'narrative critics are able to demonstrate that the intended literary effect of Matthew is not to foster anti-Semitism.'[9]

---

[8] Powell 1990, 66–67.

[9] Powell 1990, 66. Exactly the opposite, however, is proposed by Adele Reinhartz (1988). According to Reinhartz, a literary-critical reading of the gospels clearly shows that 'ideal readers,' that is, readers who assent to these narratives without critical reservation, are

Yet I wonder whether Powell, too, is not missing a point here. For while he may speak of the *literary* effect of Matthew, what he is actually referring to is the evangelist's (or, if you insist, the authorized reliable narrator's) *ideological* point of view. This is because Powell's strategy of textual analysis can only cope with two levels of meaning, that is, literary and real-world. What should be the level of ideology is missing, or falsely assimilated into the realm of the literary world. As a consequence, the ideology reflected in the text incorrectly appears as a mere literary device.[10]

At this point, another good reason for distinguishing between the realms of textuality and ideology also becomes apparent. Ideology, not unlike the everyday life it seeks to embrace, is *serious*. In (physical as well as symbolic) reality, there is no escape in saying 'Fear not, my child; it was *just a story*.' In order to recognize this seriousness, a mere formal, textual approach just may not be enough. This is because, in literary fiction, seriousness is no more intentional than it is conscious. Yet even in a fictional narrative (not to mention a non-fictional one such as Matthew), a serious, ideological level exists as distinct from the (in itself abstract) level of 'plain textuality;' what, say, *Mother Goose* implies of social class, means of production, or gender roles, is not exclusively part of the fictive world of the work, but belongs to a different discourse altogether.

Finally, for a new paradigm, Syreeni's model may not necessarily seem to be offering much that is radically new. Rather, it systematizes in general terms what has traditionally been the task of modern biblical criticism: to study the text's linguistic form, theology and historical situation.[11] Insisting that none of these is ignored, it lays down an enduring *sine qua non* of biblical studies.

---

supposed to accept the villainous role of the Jews and the negative attitudes toward them (p. 532). The gospels are, therefore, well capable of encouraging anti-Jewish attitudes if actual readers read the story as the narrative leads them to.

[10] Cf. Syreeni 1995; Merenlahti and Hakola 1999; for further discussion (that took place after this chapter was written), see Powell 2001, 119–120, 237–238. The point becomes even more obvious if we replace Matthew's gospel as subject of analysis with some typical German national socialist propaganda story from the 1930s. In that case, too, it would of course be *possible* to claim that the narrator's choice of the Jews as representatives of the moral corruption he seeks to uproot is merely a random feature of a fully respectable rhetorical strategy. Nevertheless, most of us would probably feel troubled about this interpretation.

[11] Syreeni himself is the first to admit this; see Syreeni 1997, 112, 119.

Correspondingly, the real edge of Syreeni's program lies in the critical question whether current interpretive practices actually succeed in observing the paradigm that is *already* supposed to be in force. As we have seen, this has not been the case either with the traditional historical-critical methods (that are insensitive to aspects of textuality and narrativity, and have only partially grasped the implications of viewing historical reality as a social construct), or with the more recent 'literary approaches' (that flirt with ahistorical models and fail properly to recognize aspects of ideology in texts). In both cases, the problem is that the mode of investigation applied will only account for two or less out of three relevant dimensions of texts.

In Syreeni's own analyses of biblical texts it is, as a rule, the ideological aspect that receives the greatest emphasis. Apparently, while none of the three worlds should go neglected, the most severe flaw a method can have is to ignore the ideological aspect and pay no or insufficient attention to the *mediated* nature of the link between reality and texts, and between texts and their readers. Along the *mimetic axis*, the representation of reality can only take place through ideology, a particular symbolic world; and along the *poietic axis*, on the other hand, the reader's reception and response to the text are necessarily conditioned by his or her own symbolic universe. It is for this reason that Syreeni's model deserves its epithet, '*hermeneutic.*'

Textures in a Tapestry: Vernon Robbins' Socio-Rhetorical Approach

Vernon Robbins first introduced the term 'socio-rhetorical' in a 1984 book entitled *Jesus the Teacher: A Socio-Rhetorical Interpretation of Mark.* What he was after was a method that would be sensitive to the literary and rhetorical aspects of the gospels and Acts, while also properly considering the Mediterranean society and culture in which these works originated. With the publication of the paperback edition in 1992, this initial attempt had grown into a four-arena approach that programmatically addressed *inner texture, intertexture, social and cultural texture*, and *ideological texture* in biblical interpretation. In 1996, Robbins published two systematic introductions to this approach, one in a more comprehensive, the other in a more concise form.

In a nutshell, *inner texture* concerns the intrinsic form of the text as such; its literary, aesthetic and argumentative structures and meanings.

Intertexture involves a text's configuration of language as used in its literary and social environment ('oral-scribal intertexture'); of social structures and practices ('social intertexture'); of modes of understanding and belief ('cultural intertexture') and of historical events ('historical intertexture'). *Social and cultural texture* comprise the social and cultural location of the text itself as discourse: *specific social topics* that exhibit the typical social response the text gives in the form of seven different types of social rhetoric ('conversionist,' 'revolutionist,' 'introversionist,' 'gnostic-manipulationist,' 'thaumaturgical,' 'reformist,' 'utopian');[12] *common social and cultural topics* that express 'the range of customary practices, central values, modes of relationship and exchange, perceptions about resources for life and well-being, and presuppositions about purity and taboo the text embodies;'[13] and *final cultural categories* that most decisively identify the text's cultural location – that is, the values and practices it emphasizes in a certain system of priority – in terms of five different kinds of *culture rhetoric*: 'dominant culture,' 'subculture,' 'counterculture or alternative culture,' 'contraculture or oppositional culture,' and 'liminal culture.' *Ideological texture*, finally, involves taking sides, that is, 'the way the text itself and interpreters of the text position themselves in relation to other individuals and groups' due to the particular view of people and reality the text and its interpretations evoke.[14]

Like Syreeni, so also Robbins combines his model with the originally narratological model of narrative communication, co-ordinated with a vertical, mimetic axis of representation and a horizontal, rhetorical axis of communication (see Fig. 2). What results is an extended model in which the world of the text is set into the primary context of the *Ancient Mediterranean world* (that includes a real *author* and an original *audience*,

---

[12] Here Robbins is drawing on Bryan Wilson's typology of seven types of religious sects (1963, 1969, 1973), as applied to Mark's gospel by James A. Wilde (1978).

[13] Robbins 1996b, 3; at this point, Robbins is able to incorporate in his model the work done on social-scientific criticism of the New Testament by scholars such as Bruce J. Malina, John E. Elliott, Jerome H. Neyrey, Paul W. Hollenbach, Richard L. Rohrbaugh, Carolyn Osiek, Douglas E. Oakman, John J. Pilch, Halvor Moxnes, Philip Esler, Dennis Duling, Mark McVann and others (see Robbins 1996a, 159).

[14] Robbins 1996b, 4. In Robbins 1996b, Robbins also distinguishes a fifth type of texture, namely *sacred texture* which 'exists in texts that somehow address the relation of humans to the divine . . . Sacred texture exists in communication about gods, holy persons, spirit beings, divine history, human redemption, human commitment, religious community, and ethics' (4). Apparently, this opens up the possibility for not only exegesis but also New Testament theology to be included in Robbins' interpretive model.

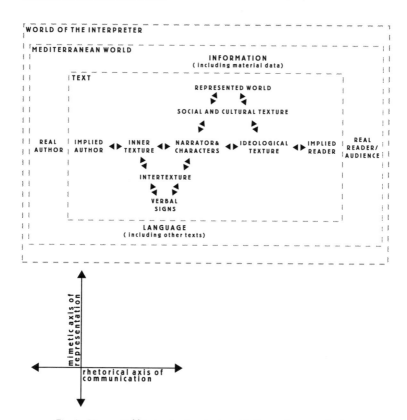

Fig. 2: Vernon Robbins' socio-rhetorical model of textual communication.

information about the realities of this world, and the historically-, socially-, culturally- and geographically-specific use of *language*) and into the secondary context of the *World of the interpreter*. The useful narratological concepts of the *implied author* and *implied reader* are joined with the idea of a text's 'implied language' manifest in *verbal signs,* and 'implied information' about the Mediterranean world *as represented in the text.* Significantly, this manoeuvre allows all four arenas of texture investigated in socio-rhetorical criticism to be identified *in the text.*[15]

---

[15] See Robbins 1996a, 20–24.

*

As a candidate for a new paradigm of New Testament studies, Robbins' system shows marked similarities to Syreeni's model. Like Syreeni, Robbins combines social-scientific and literary-rhetorical theories in the hope of attaining a new comprehensive synthesis. Moreover, like Syreeni, he is not so much proposing 'a method or theory in the usual sense,' but 'an integrated interdisciplinary environment of interpretation' or '(a step toward) broad-based interpretive analytics.'[16] In a sense, when focusing on 'values, convictions, and beliefs both in the texts we read and in the world in which we live,' Robbins may actually be thought of as embracing the three worlds of Syreeni, even to the extent that he, like Syreeni, seems to distinguish between the *symbolic world* of a particular text and the larger and more general concept of the *symbolic universe*.[17]

On the other hand, however, Robbins' model is also quite unique – just as its author is unique. To illustrate the significance of the interpreter's social and cultural location and ideology, Robbins describes his own origins as a rural farm boy, his accustomedness to manual labor, and his inclination to a mechanic's work in particular. His own conclusion is that 'Socio-rhetorical criticism is my answer to what I think I must do to perform biblical interpretation in a manner that embodies who I am.'[18]

The point is well made. Robbins' own emphasis seems to be primarily on the fact that socio-rhetorical criticism implies an interest in the concrete everyday life of 'little people,' an interest that remains an integral part of Robbins' own persona as well. However, we could also take this analogy a little further and say that socio-rhetorical criticism reminds us of a farmhouse product as well as of a mechanic's tool: it is home made from the best ingredients, and it is designed to work. For it is state-of-the-art *techniques* that Robbins uses from different, specialized fields within current New Testament study, so as to combine them into a comprehensive science of textual engineering with a focus on concrete life in societies as manifest in concrete rhetorical patterns in texts.

---

[16] Robbins 1996a, 3, 12–13, 42.
[17] Robbins 1996b, 1. Cf. Syreeni 1994, 523.
[18] Robbins 1996a, 24–27; cf. Robbins 1996b, 97–98.

Here, I think, is the strongest and at the same time the most vulnerable point of Robbins' system: it is precisely what he says it is, namely *social and rhetorical*. As such, it is highly usable and genuinely hermeneutic: it will only consider reality as *mediated* through ideology and social experience, and as *objectified* in observable rhetorical patterns of texts. On the other hand, due to this particular trimming it may not necessarily succeed in keeping its promise 'to bring disciplines into interpretation on their own terms and engage those disciplines in dialogue on an equal basis.'[19] In practice, socio-rhetorical criticism is distinctive enough a method that Robbins may casually speak of it as one.[20] As such, it will survive only through *competition* with other methods – which is enough to make us a little suspicious that its premise of dialogue and peaceful coexistence with any other approach will, in reality, turn out to be just as conditional as similar premises in so many 'dominant cultures' during the history of humanity: others may come as they are, as long as they consent to being assimilated.

The cost of assimilation is loss of original characteristics. Not all scholars, I imagine, would readily assent to conceiving of their special fields of enquiry as 'textures' of texts or functional tools for socio-rhetorical analysis. Their question might be whether Robbins' good intentions do not pave the way for a kind of methodological theme park where various approaches from entirely different environments are set together in artificial harmony.

Simplicity of construction is the real *tour de force* of Robbins' model. Each family of methods is introduced as a new plug-and-play feature to the overall system of interpretation. What emerges is a remarkably user-friendly interface for practical analysis. The other side of simplicity, however, is that the limits are always near. In Robbins' own words, his model can only help 'some people some of the time do some of the things they wish to do.'[21] The more sophisticated questions we make, the more likely the boundaries between the different 'textures' waver. For example, to what extent can the text's 'inner texture' and 'intertexture' be treated separately? Does not the inner texture depend on the meaning of terms in their cultural-temporal context? Like Syreeni's 'worlds', Robbins' 'textures' are deconstructable – and even more so, because they come more numerous and aim at greater distinction.

---

[19] Robbins 1996a, 42.
[20] Thus e.g. Robbins 1996a, 13.
[21] Robbins 1996a, 244.

Taking Poetics off Limits

Whether the models of Syreeni and Robbins finally succeed in *formulating* a new paradigm for biblical studies or not, they positively *imply* a conspicuous paradigm shift. In Syreeni's case, this takes place by demonstrating the obvious shortcomings of former dominant paradigms. Robbins, in turn, introduces an articulate method of textual analysis that aspires to be considerably more inclusive as well as concrete – and in this sense paradigmatic – than any previous one.

In terms of contents (as much as that can be formulated), the kind of paradigm implied in these models will provide an intelligible basis for recognizing the historical, social and cultural contingency of poetics. This recognition will concern, first, poetics as *primary experience* of significant form as it takes place in a particular space and time characterized by certain material, social and cultural conditions; and, second, poetics as a systematic *secondary description and assessment* of this kind of experience. What results is essentially an amplification of traditional descriptive poetics (and, by virtue of implication, narrative criticism) in the direction of hermeneutics, so as to make it a deeper (the 'vertical' aspect), wider (the 'horizontal' aspect), and more self-reflective mode of investigation than it was before.

In terms of theory, this must be considered satisfactory – which is to say that, in principle, the present study has reached its end. Yet there remains one more thing to be dealt with.

Shamefully insipid as this will sound, there is always something about poetics that remains beyond theorizing, modeling and description. Due to the distinct nature of the primary poetic experience (that which Rhoads correctly noticed to be constitutive for the identity of narrative criticism now as before), and due to the inevitable presence of this primary experience in any secondary attempt to scope it, even a relative conception of poetics as theory stumbles. Ultimately, that peculiar sense of meaningfulness in formal composition which characterizes all poetic experience (rooted in historical realities and socio-cultural meaning as that is in every case) is profoundly indeterminate. Metaphoric in essence, it escapes adequate description. Poetic meaning in the fullest sense of the word hides out of sight, beyond linguistic utterance, in a frozen, perpetual state of coming.[22]

---

[22] This is the point argued, with insurmountable rhetorical power, in Steiner 1989.

Thus, the relativity of any theory of poetics is of a radical kind. At some fundamental level, descriptive models are not so much descriptive as they are metaphoric. They each deliver a partial truth of how texts work and what they mean, *as it were*.

More than anywhere else, this metaphoric condition of all poetics is, I think, exemplified in psychoanalytic approaches to literature and art. Among approaches to human reality there are only few that can, even when taken to extremes, be as overtly imperialistic and confident of their supreme hermeneutic power as can the theory and practice of psychoanalysis. What other intellectual enterprise has the same Promethean obsession to say the unsayable, to make an image with which no idol can compare? And still (and at best, writers on psycho-analysis are lucidly aware of this), the striving of analytic practice towards expressive coherence, towards the giving of form to the essentially formless unconscious Id, is only a truth-*fiction*, an *as-if*, an instrumental metaphor.[23]

To attain the truth, we need to *re-imagine* it. To understand one story, we have to tell another. As far as it subscribes to this, psychoanalysis is a close relative to allegory and midrash. At the same time, it is also easy to see why psychoanalytic readings have acquired such a strong position in postmodern literary criticism. To say that final meanings are unconscious and can be attained only in translation gives strong support to the typically postmodernist rejection of any privileged critical discourse, to 'a suspicion of the claim to mastery that characterizes traditional readings of texts, including modern biblical scholarship.'[24] For psychoanalysis and for postmodernism, as soon as interpretation reaches the conscious, it becomes a secondary construct, contingent and incomplete. Text and its interpretations end up being on the same level hierarchically. Fiction is called forth to explain fiction.

Might psychoanalytic criticism, in its quenchless desire for finality, provide biblical criticism with a language with which to describe the poetic effect of the gospel narratives metaphorically? Moreover, could this pave the way for the conscious use of truth-fictions and instrumental metaphors as alternatives to, or as complementary with, models of relative descriptive power? This, I believe, is worth some further examination.

[23] Cf. Steiner 1989, 107–110, 173–174.
[24] The Bible and Culture Collective 1995, 2.

9

Poetics and Psychoanlaysis:
A Case for Instrumental Metaphors?

Applications of psychoanalysis to literature and art tend to provoke profound discussion concerning the role of explanatory frameworks and analytic models in the art of interpretation. On the one hand, psychoanalysis has been seen as the worst kind of example of an 'imperialist' approach that always appears to claim the monopoly of meaning, 'the final hermeneutic power.'[1] On the other hand, the theory and practice of psychoanalysis seem to testify to the limited, metaphoric nature of all secondary interpretation.

In this chapter, I will consider three different types of psychoanalytic criticism: the 'psychopoetics' of Peter Brooks, 'transactive criticism' proposed by Norman Holland and structural psychoanalytic criticism inspired by the psychoanalysis of Jacques Lacan. What unites these in many ways different theorists is the centrality they each give to the idea of correspondence between literary and psychic process – an idea essential to psychoanalytic approaches to literature in general. My question is, could this idea be 'demythologized' so that we might apply it as an *instrumental metaphor* regardless of whether we actually believe that psychoanalytic theories (of literature or of the human psyche) carry any real explanatory force? Moreover, does the nature of the psychoanalytic discourse itself, as much as it affirms the fact that no final, verifiable truth about the unconscious or about the 'Real' can be attained, not in fact suggest such a demythologization? Finally, does a similar paradox not characterize all poetics and hermeneutics: how can we describe the meaning and effect of a text comprehensively while simultaneously maintaining that this meaning and effect are distinct from, and something more than, any subsequent interpretation; that there is some undeconstructable difference between primary works and secondary readings?

---

[1] Brooks 1987, 3. On doubts in biblical scholarship concerning psychological approaches see Theissen 1987 (1983), 1.

In more concrete terms, the question is whether psychoanalytic discourse might serve as an example of how to apply a contingent, yet 'particularly insistent and demanding'[2] intertext for poetic analysis of the gospels, not so much to explain the biblical text as to thematize the interpretive condition of which both the original text and the intertext are objectifications.

From Formalism to Freud: The Psychopoetics of Peter Brooks

In his well-received book *Reading for the Plot: Design and Intention in Narrative* (1984), Peter Brooks uses 'two different models derived from Freud to talk about two different aspects of narrative.'[3] The first model is taken from Freud's *Beyond the Pleasure Principle* (1920), which Brooks transforms into a paradigm for how narratives work.

Brooks starts with the notion that narrative is an act of *repetition*. To narrate is to reproduce a sequence of events that is supposed to have taken place 'once upon a time' in the world of the story. Moreover, various narrative techniques are, essentially, techniques of repetition. Thus, when Freud says that neurotic behavior is *a compulsion to repeat* events or phantasies of the past, this makes Brooks able to conclude that, structurally, narrative and the neurosis are driven by a similar kind of force.

In *Beyond the Pleasure Principle*, Freud links this repetition compulsion to a more general, instinctual 'urge inherent in organic life to restore an earlier state of things.'[4] Ultimately, this urge will lead to a state in which the organism becomes inorganic once again, which means that, in Freud's words, 'the aim of all life is death.'[5] However, Freud also assumes that the organism's self-preserving instincts make it react to various external stimuli so that death will not take place too soon, or in 'an improper manner.' What results is – the course of life: detours and modifications that delay the end.

Similarly, says Brooks, every narrative is initially directed towards its own termination, that is, a state in which everything is said, the story is

---

[2] Cf. Brooks 1987, 17.
[3] Brooks 1984, 320; cf. Rickard 1994, 6.
[4] Freud 1920, 244. The page numbers in my footnotes refer to the *Standard Edition* (18,7) as reprinted in Freud, *The Essentials of Psycho-Analysis* (London: Penguin Books, 1991).
[5] Freud 1920, 246.

told, and the narrative has lost all of its 'narratability.'[6] Before this end can be reached, however, the narrative, too, has to resist the threat of ending too soon. As a consequence, it will produce a series of repetitions that bind its narrative energy until the point where, in an ideal case, all narratability is consummated. What results is *plot* – lifelike detours and complications that delay the end.

The second model that Brooks takes up from Freud is that of psychoanalytic *transference* which Brooks considers 'consonant with the narrative situation and the text.'[7] Like the analyst and the analysand, the reader and the text of a narrative *interact* to construct an integrated interpretation of whatever happened in the past, or at the time of the story. Notably, this interpretive construction never becomes either fully complete or objectively verifiable. Instead, narrative and transference involve – to quote Brooks – 'an unspecifiable network of event, fiction, and interpretation.'[8]

Finally, what unites Brooks' two applications of Freud is his idea of the narrative form as an expression of the typically human need to find meaning in temporal existence.[9] According to Brooks, the narrative form implies that we can learn the truth of our present situation by recovering the origins of that situation in the past. This belief is portrayed in the structure of every narrative. A narrative revives a particular chain of events, structures it and supplies it with meanings, in order to present *a retrospective explanation of its own ending*. As a result, its readers will see that what brought that ending into being was not an irrelevant series of accidents, but a genuine story. Even though the readers may realize that this vision of intentionality and integrity is fiction, it remains *reassuring fiction* that gives a sense of meaning to life in its temporality.

*

What kind of contribution might Brooks' reading of Freud make to reading the gospel narratives? First of all, his project is not without problems. Even though he says he wants to avoid 'sterile formalism,'[10] his basic starting point is nevertheless a genuine formalist one. For

---

[6] Cf. Steiner 1989, 141: 'in their terminal structure, narrations are rehearsals for death.'
[7] Brooks 1984, 320.
[8] Brooks 1984, 278.
[9] Cf. Rickard 1994, 4–5.
[10] Brooks 1994, 44.

him, narrative is still an objective category of the mind, 'one of the ways in which we speak, one of the large categories in which we think.'[11] Indeed, he believes that 'in the case of psychoanalysis, paradoxically we can go beyond formalism only by becoming more formalistic;' to find 'that desired place where literature and life converge we need to become convinced that we make our art in our own image, that the very same basic drives that determine our psychic construction also determine aesthetic form.'[12]

In Brooks' use, the word 'we' has a marked ring of universalism. What he seems to be saying is that psychoanalysis after all presents an objective as well as a universal model of the workings of the human psyche. Accordingly, a psychoanalytic model of narrative would give us an objective description of how all narratives work. What structuralist narratology once could not do, psychoanalytic literary criticism can.

Not many people would be willing to concede so much. Yet we should be able to apply Brooks' ideas in a more metaphoric sense, too. (In fact, several critics of Brooks would prefer just that.)[13] Observing the narrative form *as if* its functions paralleled (and who knows if they actually do) those of a psychic organism as conceived through psychoanalysis might then offer us inspiring insights into how gospel narratives work. In any case, observing how one narrative of considerable cultural relevance interprets another should in all probability teach us something important about each.

Evidently, the use of the narrative form enables the gospels to make meaning and establish truth in a particular way. It is also obvious that this truth is taken to reside in the primeval past; in order to recover it, the gospels present the *beginning* of the good news that Jesus' followers proclaim. As we have seen, this becomes palpable in the opening of each of the four gospels.[14]

Furthermore, the redactional work done by the evangelists resembles the situation of psychoanalytic transference. What the evangelists aimed at was integrating the diverse material they found in their oral and written sources into an organized literary and ideological whole that would suit the present faith and practices of their respective communities. This aim was somewhat similar to the aim of the classical

[11] Brooks 1984, 323.
[12] Brooks 1994, 26.
[13] See Brooks 1987, 16; Brooks 1994, 36–44.
[14] See p. 43 above.

Freudian analyst: '*Wo Es war soll Ich werden*' – the irregular impulses stemming from the past should be brought under the control of some overarching principle, so that a recognizable identity in the present might emerge. As a result, each gospel is reminiscent of an analysis session (or a series of them). Like analysis, a gospel narrative is perpetually incomplete and full of tension. Diffuse primary experience and integrated secondary interpretations combat ceaselessly within the artificial – indeed, fictive – boundaries of narrative.

Interpretation as a Function of Identity: Reading with Norman Holland

In many respects, Norman Holland's ideas of psychoanalytic criticism are in diametric opposition to those presented by Peter Brooks. Brooks believes that 'the bad name' psychoanalytic criticism 'has largely made for itself' has to do with the tendency to displace the object of analysis from the text to some person, be that person the author, the reader, or the fictive persons in the text.[15] To serve its purpose, psychoanalytic criticism should be textual and rhetorical. Holland, for his part, maintains that

> [t]he literary critic comes to psychoanalysis because psychoanalysis promises to tell him something about people. Psychoanalysis has nothing, absolutely nothing, to tell us about literature *per se*. But psychoanalysis, particularly in its theories of character, has a great deal to tell us about people engaged in literature, either writing it or reading it or being portrayed in it.[16]

On the other hand, Holland, just like Brooks, builds upon the idea of correspondence between literary and psychic process. In brief, Holland's version of this correspondence reads: 'Unity is to text as identity is to self.'[17] In his terms, the decisive correspondence prevails between *how people interact with other people and how people interact with texts*. He believes that both types of 'transactions' are governed by the participating person's personal style, that is, the unchanging personal identity that the child first establishes through its relation to its mother and later maintains through its entire adult life. Thus, the way a reader interprets

---

[15] Brooks 1987, 1–2.
[16] Holland 1982, 31.
[17] Holland 1975b, 121.

POETICS FOR THE GOSPELS?

a text corresponds to the reader's own characteristic 'identity theme' so that, ultimately, 'interpretation is a function of identity:'[18]

> The overarching principle is: identity re-creates itself, or, to put it another way, style – in the sense of personal style – creates itself. That is, all of us, as we read, use the literary work to symbolize and finally to replicate ourselves. We work through the text our own characteristic patterns of desire and adaptation. We interact with the work, making it part of our own psychic economy and making ourselves part of the literary work – as we interpret it.[19]

The meaning Holland gives to his key concepts *identity* and *interpretation* helps us to define his position. The notion of identity to which he refers originates from a distinct post-Freudian tradition, namely, *ego-psychology*.[20] Typically, ego-psychology focuses on the human self as an integrative force that maintains identity by adjusting the inner, instinctual drives of the 'id' to external prohibitions, thus helping the individual adapt to human society. When seen in this framework, literature is a subtle means of socialization that helps the people engaged in it to manage their instinctual energies and, consequently, to maintain a unified self. The aesthetic pleasure literature gives results not so much from the fulfilment of the reader's private phantasy (as Freud thought) as from the managing of this phantasy and transforming it into some socially acceptable form.

In Holland's model, the inherent unity that ego-psychology attributes to the self corresponds to another type of unity at which Holland thinks critics should arrive in literary interpretation. For him, the aim of interpretation is very much the same as it was in conventional formalist criticism: to discover the meaning of the work by showing how all its

---

[18] Holland 1975b, 123.
[19] Holland 1975b, 124. To find empirical support for his thesis, Holland put up an experimental program the results of which are described in Holland 1975a: he recorded and analyzed interviews of students' responses to William Faulkner's 'A Rose for Emily' and discovered that these responses conformed to the readers' personality profiles as shown in standard psychological tests. Holland has reiterated his thesis in a vast number of publications over the last two decades.
[20] Among the founders of ego-psychology are Ernst Kris, Heinz Hartmann, Rudolph Loewenstein, and Erik Erikson. In his early works, especially in Holland 1968, Holland builds on the basis of Freud 1908, but is also strongly influenced by the theories of Kris. The notion of identity presupposed in Holland 1975b derives from Heinz Lichtenstein, whom Holland introduces as 'the most precise of the modern theorists of identity' (p. 120). For an assessment of ego-psychological contributions to literary criticism, see Wright 1984, 56–68.

elements relate to one central theme. Consequently, even though he speaks emphatically of 'the dynamics of literary response,'[21] the type of comparison he makes of text to self has been criticized for merely transforming a static, formalist notion of text fully intact into a static, essentialist notion of the self.[22]

*

Those who have criticized Holland do, I think, have a point. There is no reason to believe that our texts are any more unified than we are.[23]

On the other hand, to view interpretation as a function of identity might still be rewarding. While our texts as well as our selves may well be liable to division and deconstruction, the *conventions* of unity of texts and of assurance of the self have a strong enough history of dominance to make a comparison between them interesting. Even as a similarity of two corresponding fictions, this just might turn out to be informative.

In any case, a particular, *de facto* ego-psychological view of interpretation as a function of identity seems to be an unspoken assumption in quite a few exegetical studies already. As such, it is a fine case of how deeply Freudian discourse has naturalized itself within our speech and modes of thinking.[24]

Take the widely accepted idea of 'Deuteronomist theology' for example. This theology is suggested to have motivated the final redaction of the so-called *Deuteronomic History Work* in the Hebrew Bible.[25] The core idea expressed in Deuteronomist theology is that the destruction of Jerusalem in the year 587 BCE was not a sign of failure of the God of Israel, but God's premeditated punishment of the infidelity of his chosen people.

In scholarship, Deuteronomist theology is generally considered an attempt to master an acute *identity crisis*. It enabled the Judeans to

---

[21] This is the title of Holland 1968, the book that begins his project.
[22] Thus e.g. Freund 1987, 125: 'In effect his strategy . . . is to shift the unity and self-identity, traditionally attributed to the autonomous text, from the literary work to the text of a reader's "self."'
[23] Moore 1994, 74–81.
[24] Cf. Freund 1987, 132.
[25] The theory of the Deuteronomi(sti)c History Work (Deut., Josh., Judg., 1–2 Sam., 1–2 Kgs) and the ideology behind it originated with the publication of Martin Noth's *Überlieferungsgeschichtliche Studien* in 1943 (Engl. trans. 1981).

interpret a national catastrophe so that the national religion and, consequently, national identity need not be rejected. In other words, it helped the Judean collective self to defend its integrity in the face of external pressure.

On the New Testament side, questions concerning the way the human self deals with the threat of disintegration seem equally pertinent. For early Christianity, conflict with and departure from 1st-century Judaism constituted a case of identity crisis. While the first followers of Jesus held fast to their traditional Jewish identity, a gradually growing number of newcomers saw the 'Old Israel' as being replaced by a 'New Israel,' a new constitution of the Chosen People with an entirely new kind of covenant with God. What resulted were conflicts, traces of which can be detected in various New Testament writings. Paul's Letter to the Galatians, for example, is a direct witness of one such conflict.

As to the more specific issue of reading as a function of identity, the gospel narratives do, I think, present a suggestive case. After all, the gospels are readings. Studies of their origins indicate that they were composed so as to interpret other texts and traditions that the evangelists used as their sources. During a process of redaction, each evangelist sought to subordinate earlier material to his own fresh narrative and ideological vision. In an ideal case, this vision would be *a formal and conceptual unity that would match a particular idea of Christian identity*, typical of the community in which the gospel in question originated. Thus, the process of redaction might be seen as a process of '*textual socialization*,' that is, adaptation of texts, traditions, and their ideologies to external norms and expectations. These norms and expectations could have been ideological – the theological content of a true Christian gospel should be such and such – or literary: a gospel should (or should not) resemble this or that known literary genre or text type. In either case, the way the text of a gospel, as a particular reading of early Christian tradition, reaches towards integrity matches the psychosocial efforts (be they epistemologically well grounded or not) of those people among whom the text originated.

The Necessity of Absence: Jacques Lacan's Structural Psychoanalysis

The models of Brooks and Holland draw upon the idea of a correspondence between literary and psychic process. In this respect, these two models are by no means unique. On the contrary, most psychoanalytic readings of literature since Freud have, at least implicitly, assumed a similar type of correspondence.[26] The most radical and by far also the most influential version of this idea is presented by the tradition of *structural psychoanalytic criticism*. This tradition relates, most notably, to the reinterpretation of Freud proposed by Jacques Lacan.[27]

For Lacan, language and textuality play a crucial role in the creation of the unconscious, whereas the unconscious, in turn, resides very much in the structure of language. It is the very experience of language that causes the individual subject to split into the conscious and the unconscious.

At a pre-linguistic stage, says Lacan, the child maintains an illusion of the absolute, enduring presence of the mother as a source of immediate satisfaction. Lacan calls this stage the realm of the *Imaginary*. When the child gains access to language, the illusion previously held breaks up. From the realm of the Imaginary the child enters the rule of the *Symbolic*. Expected to express her desire in articulate words, the child understands that desire is not met with satisfaction automatically. According to Lacan, this causes what Freud called *primal repression*: ideas attached to instincts are denied entrance into the conscious; as a result, the unconscious comes into being.

Lacan draws upon Ferdinand de Saussure, the father of structural linguistics, who regarded the sign as a combination of two elements, a *signifier* and a *signified*. A signifier is a distinct word-sound, a signified a concept the word-sound stands for. According to de Saussure, the link between the two is entirely arbitrary; any word-sound can be linked with any concept. Once the link is made, however, he took it to be firm and secure. In his terms, the signifier and the signified are as inseparable as the two sides of a sheet of paper.[28]

---

[26] Lionel Trilling (1961) was the first to make this connection explicit. After Freud, most psychoanalytic readings of literature had focused predominantly on the author's psychic processes. At the same time, however, they had also given attention to how these processes were *figured in the text*, thus anticipating an openly textual and rhetorical approach. (See Wright 1984, 36; Freund 1987, 131.)

[27] For a concise introduction to Lacan's ideas, see e.g. Richardson 1983; Wright 1984, 107–132; from the point of view of biblical studies, The Bible and Culture Collective 1995, 196–211; Schwall 1997. My own presentation here is based mainly on these secondary introductions, as well as on Lacan 1977, an English selection from Lacan 1966. While books on Lacan written by other people abound, his doctoral dissertation was the only book he himself published until he was 65. Then, in 1966, *Écrits*, a massive collection of papers appeared. Instead of books, Lacan's major contribution was the oral teaching he gave in his famous seminar.

[28] de Saussure 1977 (1915), 113.

In Lacan's view, on the other hand, the link between the signifier and the signified is not secure at all. This is because the identification of the signified is, ultimately, a matter of human judgment. Thus, contrary to what de Saussure said, any given signifier does not correspond to some one signified. Rather, signifiers signify other signifiers that signify other signifiers, and so on, *ad infinitum*. On the level of the conscious, then, language operates like an endless chain of words in which each word signals the absence of what it stands for. This absence keeps frustrating the unconscious wherein the desire for immediate satisfaction – that is, a symbiotic union of signifiers and signifieds – still lives in exile.

Thus – and this is worth noting – the Symbolic never succeeds in taking over completely; here Lacan's reading of Freud differs markedly from the notion of ego-psychology. While ego-psychology postulates a unified identity that is taken to be the result of the ego's success in its 'progressive conquest of the id,'[29] Lacan introduces a notion of *a divided subject* permanently split into two parts, an ego that recognizes the inevitable absence of satisfaction, and an unconscious that keeps reaching out after its lost objects of desire. In Lacan's own terms, the Imaginary and the Symbolic compete ceaselessly for control over the unattainable *Real.*

*

While Lacan's own readings of literature have inspired a great number of commentators, the main effect of his work has been felt not so much in critical praxis as in the field of literary theory.[30] Correspondingly, in Lacan's case the use of psychoanalysis as an intertext rather than a method comes most naturally. This is all the more so because in certain respects, there seems to be quite a close family resemblance between Lacan's thought and that of the evangelists. In particular, this concerns the idea of *the absence of meaning.*

A number of paradigmatic Biblical passages emphasize the utmost importance of understanding correctly *the true, hidden meaning* of what one sees or hears. Above, in chapter four, I pointed out three such

---

[29] Freud 1923, 56.
[30] Lacan's famous 'Seminar on Edgar Allan Poe's *The Purloined Letter*' (1972, orig. publ. in Lacan 1966) gives an idea of how Lacan approached a literary text.

passages as archetypal cases in point, namely, the Markan Parable Theory, the Johannine Misunderstandings, and the encounter of Philip and the Ethiopian official in the Acts of the Apostles.[31]

According to the Markan Parable Theory (Mark 4:10–12), Jesus' parables are riddles whose true sense can be attained only by means of interpretation. The Johannine misunderstandings involve a confusion of the literal and the spiritual sense: people think that Jesus is speaking of earthly things, when, in fact, he is speaking of the heavenly (John 3:12). In Acts 8:26–40, the Ethiopian court official learns that understanding the Scriptures is only possible by gaining access to the way insiders read. Essentially, all these episodes reach beyond appearances and representations – that is, beyond the Imaginary and the Symbolic – to the realm of the secret gospel truth: the Real. Because the Real resides beyond the letter, it is of necessity unspeakable. As a consequence, words are denied their literal sense and are taken as enigmas. Instead of using literal language, the gospels are forced to apply figurative speech, parables and metaphors. The trouble is, as shown in all these passages to which I have referred as examples, that this mode of speech makes the message incomprehensible. Unless they are given the key to the correct interpretation, the Ethiopian cannot understand what he is read-ing, the disciples have to ask Jesus to explain his parables, and Jesus' audience in John is bound to perform one act of misunderstanding after another.

On the other hand, however, the correct interpretation, if given, will only take us all the way back to the realm of the Symbolic. The attempt to bypass the signifier and reach the signified only results in adding one more signifier to an infinite chain of signifiers. The signified, the Real, the object of desire, remains lost. Boldly, however, the gospels continue their quest, even though their frustrated attempts to formulate their desire in terms of language repeatedly render their mission impossible. In this sense, the gospels speak in the language of the unconscious. Words of absence are their native tongue.

*

What makes the typically psychoanalytic idea of correspondence between operations of the human mind and operations of texts produced by the

[31] Cf. above, pp. 48–55.

human mind interesting is not so much the possible verity as the very possibility of such comparison. As historical objectifications of meaning, biblical discourse and psychoanalytic discourse can communicate with each other in a meaningful way. At least at first glance, the fruits of this communication are of great promise: psychoanalytic discourse appears to be 'deeply engaged in many of the same issues that pervade the biblical texts.'[32] The case of Lacan is particularly informative and has direct relevance to biblical studies. A stereoptical (Peter Brooks' term) reading of Lacan and the gospels can shed light on how that which is primary in a text (as well as in reality) is bound to remain inarticulate. This is made thematic in the narratives of the gospels, as they repeatedly turn into secondary commentaries of their own message, suggesting that real meaning does not dwell in texts made with human hands.

[32] The Bible and Culture Collective 1995, 222.

10

Conclusion: Poetics as Myth and Fiction

In the two preceding chapters I argued that, in poetic analyses of the gospels, both descriptive models and instrumental metaphors are applicable. The former are restricted in that, while they should strive to be as comprehensive as possible, they none the less must always admit to being limited and relative, historical and cultural. As to the latter, in turn, their limits and relativity should be obvious to anyone.

The difference between these two modes of poetics as critical, secondary discourse may be compared to the difference between myth and fiction: whereas a myth is believed to be capable of actually revealing truth, a fiction is only expected to give us a sense of meaningfulness.[1] Which one we choose is no trivial decision, for both approaches have their ethical implications.

The use of models, however limited and relative they may be, contributes to the Enlightenment's project for more adequate knowledge and better historical understanding. As such, it comes with the essentially *serious* question 'Are we reading the text as accurately as we could?' A bad model is not only technically but also morally invalid. Intentionally or not, it lies to honest people who can only act according to their best knowledge.

In the case of biblical texts in particular, this question remains as urgent as ever. A considerable number of people regard the Bible not only as a canon of texts but also as a code of life. They will act on their understanding of the text. While I will not venture to suggest that critical scholarship set the norm of how Christians should read their Scripture – biblical hermeneutics is certainly a far more complex issue than that – I do think that a critical understanding of the biblical text and its contexts, acquired by scholarship, should contribute to the critical

---

[1] I am here drawing upon Frank Kermode's reflections on the nature of fiction in Kermode 1967. See esp. chap. II, *Fictions* (pp. 35–64).

evaluation of every cultural phenomenon and social practice that claims to be 'biblical.'

Moreover, even for people other than Bible-observing Christians, the Bible is part of history, and history, be it one's own or somebody else's, always comes with an obligation. History should, as far as possible, be neither forgotten nor falsely interpreted. In our human world, honor, justice, learning and, last but not least, identity, all depend on memory. 'How was it?' we ask, and then we remember who these people were, what was the right thing to do, whose fathers and grandfathers were innocent after all, and to whom we still owe our respect. It is the memory of the past that constitutes the present.

This being the case, biblical criticism has little choice but to remain serious business. It must seek the truth (a truth, some truth) about the text, whatever that might mean and how hopeless a task in the end. Because (and I hope to have shown this rather conclusively in the first two parts of this book) the formal configuration of biblical texts is not to be dissociated from their ideological meaning and intent, or from their historical and cultural environment, this responsibility concerns their poetic analysis as well.

On the other hand, even though responsible critics cannot operate with fictions and metaphors only, they cannot really avoid them in the end. While it is to be hoped that evolving methods and paradigms succeed in approaching (some relative) truth about how texts work (under certain conditions) and what they mean (to certain people), it is nevertheless only *approximation* that they may speak of. The myths of comprehensive description and final meaning remain untrue beliefs. It is in persistent opposition to this fact that human understanding goes by the name of *comprehension*. For however inadequate they may be, fictions of complete circumscription are necessary for us. We contrive synthetic totalities and proceed to operate with them, rather than with the chaotic abyss to which the world would regress without them. Obviously, such visions of wholeness are also necessary so that texts can be produced, read and understood. But while texts – original fictions – may represent an attempt to replace chaos by cosmos, they can only result in reproducing chaos in the end. Later, readings and interpretations will do the same in turn. What they perceive in texts – that is, structure and meaning – they do not discover but construct. Finally, because no text or no meaning can ever be exhausted by any reading, readings will also deconstruct – which will only give birth to new, competing 'comprehensive' visions. (There still is no scholarly consensus concerning, for example, the general structural outline of Mark's gospel.)[2] In Wallace Stevens' words, 'the final belief must be in a fiction,' that is, in 'something we know does not exist, but which helps us to make sense of and to move in the world.'[3] Ultimately, this seems to concern our interpretations of the alternative, possible worlds of texts as well.

The contradiction here is as evident as it is inevitable. It is essential that we seek the truth; in the search for truth, mere fiction will not suffice; yet there is only fiction available. We need to understand; yet we cannot.

One possible way out (not a bad one at all, I think) would be to follow the example of the natural sciences which, after the introduction of the principles of 'indeterminacy' and 'complementarity' through the quantum theory, have found themselves in a somewhat similar type of dilemma.[4] We could then consider descriptive models of texts, and the unwarranted Cartesian optimism they may imply, in some-what the same way as modern physics considers classical Newtonian mechanics: although the latter does not give a full picture of how things really are, it still works in rough figures. Correspondingly, while all talk about 'real' properties and effects (not to mention 'nature') of texts may eventually be haunted by epistemological problems, the practical difference between plausible and far-fetched readings still remains meaningful *often enough*. (There are indeed many things about the gospel of Mark on which scholars do agree.) The innermost nature of interpretive models as pragmatic fiction does not empty them of *all* descriptive power.

On the other hand, the shadow of totality, the presence of immediate satisfaction, the sense of full meaning can only be grasped in its opposite. It is only in the open singularity of some outspokenly partial readings – psychoanalytic, allegoric, perhaps also autobiographical (a recent major trend)[5] – that we may hope to find out, intuitively, what it must be like to reach a conclusive interpretation. Moreover, it is only via such thoroughly demythologized readings with an anatomy and historical and ideological conditions made visible for anyone to observe

---

[2] Cf. Dewey 1991; Dewey 1989, 40.
[3] Kermode 1967, 39.
[4] The analogy is also noted by Steiner (1989, 70–77, 125); cf. Kermode 1967, 59–63.
[5] See e.g. Staley 1999 as well as Vol. 72 (1995) of the periodical *Semeia*.

that we may venture to dream of any fulfilment at all, lest anyone should stumble and fall into the damnation of false assurance.

Of course, we must not forget that then we are only dreaming. While all descriptive models are *to some extent* metaphoric, no deliberate interpretive fiction is *anything else but* metaphoric. There is no limit to the potential structures and meanings such fictions can invoke from original texts; yet all those structures and meanings are mutually inter-changeable. Although each of them can show the text in a new and illuminating light, or give it one more language in which to speak to us, none of them will be any more true than any other – or indeed, true at all. Beyond proof and disconfirmation, they merely dream of truth, putting no serious effort into finding it. Here, then, emerges a difference: while serious searchers, too, may be dreamers by nature, to dream will not be enough for them. They grieve for every hypothesis they have to drop.

Thus, and let this be the final interpretation proposed in this work, the full formula of historical poetics – strictly speaking, poetics coming of age – is made of myth and fiction as *complements* of each other. On the one hand, the Enlightenment's project for the evolution of knowledge must go on. In terms of poetics, this means that textuality and aesthetics must be properly connected with social reality liable to ongoing historical change. A poetic analysis can only work as part of a general interpretive framework or paradigm that enables this. On the other hand, the concrete practices of such analysis will inevitably turn out to be more and more particular. Compare particle physics: the more precise and evolved the analysis, the more significant the interference by the process of observation with the observed material. The more aware we are of the historicity and social nature of language, the better we will also realize the particularity of our own responses to the gospels as forms of poetic significance – even if such responses are of a systematic nature. For each poetic experience, even when drawing on some premeditated interpretive framework (and precisely then), will remain in various and peculiar ways dependent on a distinct time and place, a distinct way of seeing, and last but not least, a distinct individual work observed. As such, it will make a contribution to a vast dialogue, the meaningfulness of which will be lessened neither by the great number of voices heard nor by the uniqueness of each voice presented.

Bibliography

The abbreviations of periodicals and serials follow the
Journal of Biblical Literature Instructions for Contributors as presented at
http://www.sbl-site.org/scripts/SBL/Publications/SBL-pubs-JBL-inst.html
(update 9/20/99).

ÅGREN, G. 1996 *Rakentaja.* Finnish trans. C. Westerberg. Helsinki: Werner Söderström Osakeyhtiö.

AICHELE, G. 1996 *Jesus Framed.* New York: Routledge.

ALTER, R. 1981 *The Art of Biblical Narrative.* New York: Basic Books.

AUERBACH, E. 1953 (1946) *Mimesis: The Representation of Reality in Western Literature.* Trans. W. R. Trask. Princeton: Princeton University Press.

AUNE, D. E. 1983 *Prophecy in Early Christianity and the Ancient Mediterranean World.* Grand Rapids: Eerdmans.

BAKHTIN, M. 1984 (1963) *Problems of Dostoevsky's Poetics.* Ed. and. trans. C. Emerson. Minneapolis: University of Minnesota Press.

BAL, M. 1977 *Narratologie. Essais sur la signification narrative dans quatre romans modernes.* Paris: Klincksieck.

—— 1985 (1980) *Narratology: Introduction to the Theory of Narrative.* Trans. C. van Boheemen. Toronto: University of Toronto Press.

—— 1986 *Femmes imaginaires: L'ancien testament au risque d'une narratologie critique.* Uthrecht: HES; Montreal: HMH; Paris: Nizet.

—— 1987 *Lethal Love: Feminist Literary Readings of Biblical Love Stories.* Bloomington and Indianapolis: Indiana University Press.

—— 1988a *Death and Dissymmetry: The Politics of Coherence in the Book of Judges.* Chicago: University of Chicago Press.

—— 1988b *Murder and Difference: Gender, Genre, and Scholarship on Sisera's Death.* Bloomington: Indiana University Press.

—— 1991 *On Story-Telling: Essays in Narratology.* Ed. D. Jobling. Sonoma: Polebridge.

BARTHES, R. 1966 'Introduction à l'analyse structurale des récits.' *Communications* 8.

—— 1974 (1970) *S/Z.* Trans. R. Miller. New York: Hill & Wang.

BERGER, P. L., and LUCKMANN, TH. 1967 *The Social Construction of Reality: A Treatise in the Sociology of Knowledge.* London: Allen Lane.

BERLIN, A. 1983 *Poetics and Interpretation of Biblical Narrative*. Sheffield: Almond.

THE BIBLE AND CULTURE COLLECTIVE 1995 *The Postmodern Bible*. New Haven: Yale University Press.

BILEZIKIAN, G. G. 1977 *The Liberated Gospel: A Comparison of the Gospel of Mark and Greek Tragedy*. Grand Rapids: Baker.

BLOOM, H. 1979 'The Breaking of Form.' H. Bloom *et al.* (eds), *Deconstruction and Criticism*. London: Routledge & Kegan Paul.

BOOMERSHINE, TH. E. 1974 'Mark, the Storyteller: A Rhetorical-Critical Investigation of Mark's Passion and Resurrection Narrative.' Ph.D. diss., Union Theological Seminary, New York.

BOOTH, W. C. 1961 *The Rhetoric of Fiction*. Chicago: University of Chicago Press. (2nd edn 1983.)

—— 1974 *A Rhetoric of Irony*. Chicago: University of Chicago Press.

—— 1988 *The Company We Keep: An Ethics of Fiction*. Berkeley, Los Angeles and London: University of California Press.

BORING, M. E. 1982 *Sayings of the Risen Jesus: Christian Prophecy in the Synoptic Tradition*. Cambridge: Cambridge University Press.

BORNKAMM, G. 1963 'End-expectation and Church in Matthew.' G. Bornkamm, G. Barth, and H. J. Held (eds), *Tradition and Interpretation in Matthew*. Philadelphia: Westminister.

BROOKS, P. 1984 *Reading for the Plot: Design and Intention in Narrative*. Oxford: Clarendon Press.

—— 1987 'The idea of psychoanalytic literary criticism.' S. Rimmon-Kenan (ed.), *Discourse in Psychoanalysis and Literature*. London: Methuen.

—— 1994 *Psychoanalysis and Storytelling*. Oxford: Blackwell.

BROWN, R. E. 1966 *The Gospel According to John (I–XII)*. AB 29. New York: Doubleday.

BUBAR, W. W. 1995 'Killing Two Birds with One Stone: The Utter De(con)struction of Matthew and His Church.' *Biblical Interpretation* 3.

BULTMANN, R. 1968 (1931) *The History of the Synoptic Tradition*. Second edition with corrections and with additions from the 1962 Supplement. Trans. J. Marsh. Oxford: Basil Blackwell.

BURNETT, F. W. 1991 'The Undecidability of the Proper Name "Jesus" in Matthew.' *Semeia* 54.

—— 1994 'Characterization and Reader Construction of Characters in the Gospels.' *Semeia* 63.

BURRIDGE, R. A. 1992 *What Are the Gospels? A Comparison with Graeco–Roman Biography.* SNTSMS 70. Cambridge: Cambridge University Press.

CALINESCU, M. 1993 *Rereading.* New Haven: Yale University Press.

CAMERY-HOGGATT, J. A. 1992 *Irony in Mark's Gospel: Text and Subtext.* SNTSMS 72. Cambridge: Cambridge University Press.

CHATMAN, S. 1978 *Story and Discourse: Narrative Structure in Fiction and Film.* Ithaca: Cornell University Press.

COHN, D. 1990 'Signposts of Fictionality: A Narratological Perspective.' *Poetics Today* 11.

COLLINS, A. Y. 1992 *The Beginning of the Gospel: Probings of Mark in Context.* Minneapolis: Fortress Press.

—— 1995 'Apocalyptic Rhetoric in Social Context.' An unpublished paper presented in the SNTS 50th General Meeting in Prague.

CONZELMANN, H. 1969 (1968) *An Outline of the Theology of the New Testament.* Trans. J. Bowden. London: SCM Press.

—— 1982 (1957) *The Theology of St. Luke.* Trans. Geoffrey Buswell. Philadelphia: Fortress Press.

—— 1987 (1972) *A Commentary on the Acts of the Apostles.* Trans. J. Limburg, A. Th. Kraabel, and D. H. Juel. (Ed.) E. J. Epp with C. R. Matthews. Philadelphia: Fortress Press.

CRANE, R. S. 1952 'The Concept of Plot and the Plot of Tom Jones.' R. S. Crane (ed.), *Critics and Criticism: Ancient and Modern.* Chicago: University of Chicago Press.

CROSSAN, J. D. 1998 *The Birth of Christianity: Discovering What Happened in the Years Immediately after the Execution of Jesus.* San Francisco: HarperSanFrancisco.

CULLER, J. 1975 *Structuralist Poetics: Structuralism, Linguistics and the Study of Literature.* London: Routledge & Kegan Paul.

CULPEPPER, R. A. 1983 *Anatomy of the Fourth Gospel: A Study in Literary Design.* Philadelphia: Fortress Press.

CURRIE , G. 1990 *The Nature of Fiction.* Cambridge: Cambridge University Press.

DARR, J. A. 1992 *On Character Building: The Reader and the Rhetoric of Characterization in Luke–Acts.* Louisville: Westminister/John Knox Press.

DARR, J. A. 1993 'Narrator as Character: Mapping a Reader-Oriented Approach to Narration in Luke–Acts.' *Semeia* 63.

—— 1994 '"Watch How You Listen" (Luke 8:18): Jesus and the Rhetoric of Perception in Luke–Acts.' Malbon and McKnight (eds) 1994.

DAWSEY, J. M. 1986 *The Lukan Voice: Confusion and Irony in the Gospel of Luke.* Macon: Mercer University Press.

DEWEY, J. 1980 *Markan Public Debate: Literary Technique, Concentric Structure, and Theology in Mark 2:1–3:6.* SBLDS 48. Chico: Scholars Press.

—— 1985 'The Literary Structure of the Controversy Stories in Mark 2:1–3:6.' W. Telford (ed.), *The Interpretation of Mark.* IRT 7. London: SPCK.

—— 1989 'Oral Methods of Structuring Narrative in Mark.' *Int* 53.

—— 1991 'Mark as Interwoven Tapestry: Forecasts and Echoes for a Listening Audience.' *CBQ* 53.

—— 1994 'The Gospel of Mark as an Oral-Aural Event: Implications for Interpretation.' Malbon and McKnight (eds) 1994.

VON DOBSCHÜTZ, E. 1928 'Zur Erzählerkunst der Markus.' *ZNW* 27.

DONAHUE, J. R. 1978 'Jesus as the Parable of God in the Gospel of Mark.' *Int* 32.

—— 1994 'Redaction Criticism: Has the *Hauptstrasse* Become a *Sackgasse*?' Malbon and McKnight (eds) 1994.

DRURY, J. 1987 'Luke.' R. Alter and F. Kermode (eds), *The Literary Guide to the Bible.* Cambridge: The Belknap Press of Harvard University Press.

EAGLETON, T. 1983 *Literary Theory: An Introduction.* Oxford: Basil Blackwell.

EASTHOPE, A. 1991 *Literary into Cultural Studies.* London and New York: Routledge.

EDWARDS, J. R. 1989 'Markan sandwiches: the significance of interpolations in Markan narratives.' *NovT* 31.

EDWARDS, R. A. 1976 *A Theology of Q.* Philadelphia: Fortress Press.

ERICKSON, R. A. 1997 *The Language of the Heart: 1600–1750.* Philadelphia: University of Pennsylvania Press.

ESLER, P. F. 1987 *Community and Gospel in Luke–Acts.* Cambridge: Cambridge University Press.

FELPERIN, H. 1985 *Beyond Deconstruction: The Uses and Abuses of Literary Theory*. Oxford: Clarendon Press.

FISH, S. E. 1980 *Is There a Text in This Class? The Authority of Interpretive Communities*. Cambridge: Harvard University Press.

FONTAINE, C. 1979 'The Use of the Traditional Saying in the Old Testament.' Ph.D. diss., Duke University, Philadelphia.

FOWLER, R. M. 1991 *Let the Reader Understand: Reader-Response Criticism and the Gospel of Mark*. Minneapolis: Fortress Press.

FREUD, S. 1953 *The Standard Edition of the Complete Psychological Works* (24 vols). London: The Hogarth Press and the Institute of Psycho-analysis:

(1908) 'Creative writers and day-dreaming,' IX, 141–154;

(1920) *Beyond the Pleasure Principle,* XVIII, 1–64;

(1923) *The Ego and The Id,* XIX, 1–66.

FREUND, E. 1987 *The Return of the Reader: Reader-response criticism*. London: Methuen.

FREYTAG, G. 1894 (1863) *Technique of the Drama*. Trans. E. J. McEwan. Chicago: Scott.

FRIEDMAN, N. 1955 'Forms of the Plot.' *Journal of General Education* 8.

FUNK, R. W. 1978 'The Form of the New Testament Healing Miracle Story.' *Semeia* 12.

—— 1988 *The Poetics of Biblical Narrative*. Sonoma: Polebridge Press.

GENETTE, G. 1980 (1972) *Narrative Discourse: An Essay in Method*. Trans. J. E. Lewin. Ithaca: Cornell University Press.

—— 1993 (1991) *Fiction & Diction*. Trans. Catherine Porter. Ithaca and London: Cornell University Press.

GIBLIN, C. H. 1985 *The Destruction of Jerusalem According to Luke's Gospel: A Historical-Typological Moral*. Rome: Biblical Institute.

GRAHAM, S. L. 1991 'Silent Voices: Women in the Gospel of Mark.' *Semeia* 54.

GREENBLATT, S. 1980 *Renaissance Self-Fashioning: From More to Shakespeare*. Chicago: University of Chicago Press.

—— 1988 *Shakespearean Negotiations: The Circulation of Social Energy in Renaissance England*. Berkeley and Los Angeles: University of California Press.

GREIMAS, A. J. 1966 *Sémantique structurale: Recherche de méthode*. Paris: Larousse.

GROSSBERG, L., NELSON, C. and TREICHLER, P. A. (eds) 1992 *Cultural Studies.* New York and London: Routledge.

GRUNDMANN, W. 1963 *Das Evangelium nach Markus.* THKNT 2. 3rd edn. Berlin: Evangelische Verlagsanstalt.

HEATH, M. F. 1987 *The Poetics of Greek Tragedy.* London: Gerald Duckworth.

—— 1989 *Unity in Greek Poetics.* Oxford: Clarendon Press.

HOCK, R. F., CHANCE, J. B., and PERKINS, J. (eds) 1999 *Ancient Fiction and Early Christian Narrative.* Atlanta: Scholars Press.

HOLLAND, N. N. 1968 *The Dynamics of Literary Response.* New York: Oxford University Press.

—— 1975a *Five Readers Reading.* New Haven: Yale University Press.

—— 1975b 'Unity Identity Text Self.' Proceedings of the Modern Language Association 90; reprinted in J. P. Tompkins (ed.), *Reader-Response Criticism: From Formalism to Post-Structuralism.* Baltimore: The Johns Hopkins University Press, 1980.

—— 1982 'Why this is transference, nor am I out of it.' *Psychoanalysis and Contemporary Thought* 5.

HOLZMANN, H. 1901 *Die Synoptiker.* HNT 1. 5th edn. Tübingen und Leipzig: Mohr.

ISER, W. 1974 (1972) *The Implied Reader: Patterns of Communication in Prose Fiction from Bunyan to Beckett.* Baltimore: The Johns Hopkins University Press.

JAUSS, H. R. 1982 *Toward an Aesthetic of Reception.* Trans. T. Bahti. Minneapolis: University of Minnesota Press.

JEREMIAS, J. 1966 *The Eucharistic Words of Jesus.* Trans. N. Perrin. London: SCM Press.

JOBLING, D. 1990 'Writing the Wrongs of the World: The Deconstruction of the Biblical Text in the Context of Liberation Theologies.' *Semeia* 51.

—— 1992 'Deconstruction and the Political Analysis of Biblical Texts: A Jamesonian Reading of Psalm 72.' *Semeia* 59.

JONES, M. 1996 'A Bachtinian Approach to the Gospels: the Problem of Authority.' *Scando-Slavica, Tomus 42.*

KÄSEMANN, E. 1969 *New Testament Questions of Today.* London: SCM Press.

KELBER, W. H. (ed.) 1976 *The Passion in Mark: Studies on Mark 14–16.* Philadelphia: Fortress Press.

—— 1983 *The Oral and the Written Gospel. The Hermeneutics of Speaking and Writing in the Synoptic Tradition, Mark, Paul, and Q.* Philadelphia: Fortress Press.

—— 1988 'Narrative and Disclosure: Mechanisms of Concealing, Revealing, and Reveiling.' *Semeia* 43.

KERMODE, F. 1967 *The Sense of an Ending: Studies in the Theory of Fiction.* New York: Oxford University Press.

—— 1979 *The Genesis of Secrecy: On the Interpretation of Narrative.* Cambridge: Harvard University Press.

—— 1988 *History and Value.* Oxford: Clarendon Press.

KINGSBURY, J. D. 1986 *Matthew as Story.* Philadelphia: Fortress Press.

KLOSTERMANN, E. 1950 *Das Markusevangelium.* HNT 3. 4th edn. Tübingen: Mohr (Siebeck).

KOESTER, H. 1971 'One Jesus and Four Primitive Gospels.' Robinson and Koester 1971.

LACAN, J. 1966 *Ecrits.* Paris: Seuil.

—— 1972 'Seminar on "The Purloined Letter."' Trans. J. Mehlman. *Yale French Studies* 40.

—— 1977 *Ecrits: A Selection.* Trans. A. Sheridan. New York: Norton.

LEITCH, V. B. 1988 *American Literary Criticism from the Thirties to the Eighties.* New York: Columbia University Press.

LEVINE, G. 1994 'Introduction: Reclaiming the Aesthetic.' Levine, G. (ed.), *Aesthetics and Ideology.* New Brunswick: Rutgers University Press.

LOMBARDI-SATRIANI, L. 1975 'Folklore as a Culture of Contestation.' *Journal of the Folklore Institute* XI:1/2. The Hague: Mouton.

LÜHRMANN, D. 1987 *Das Markusevangelium.* HNT 3. Tübingen: Mohr (Siebeck).

MALBON, E. S. 1992 'Narrative Criticism: How Does the Story Mean?' J. C. Anderson and S. D. Moore (eds), *Mark & Method. New Approaches in Biblical Studies.* Minneapolis: Augsburg Fortress.

—— 1996 'The Beginning of a Narrative Commentary on the Gospel of Mark.' SBLSP.

MALBON, E. S. and McKNIGHT, E. V. (eds) 1994 *The New Literary Criticism and the New Testament*. Valley Forge: Trinity Press International; originally published by JSOT Press, Sheffield, England.

MAMET, D. 1994 *A Whore's Profession: Notes and Essays*. London and Boston: Faber & Faber.

MARCUS, J. 1992 'The Jewish War and the Sitz im Leben of Mark.' *JBL* III/3.

—— 1995 'Glimpses into the History of the Marcan Community: Mark 13:9–13 and Related Passages.' An unpublished paper presented in the SNTS 50th General Meeting in Prague.

MARSHALL, C. D. 1989 *Faith as a Theme in Mark's Narrative*. SNTSMS 64. Cambridge: Cambridge University Press.

MARTIN, W. 1986 *Recent Theories of Narrative*. Ithaca: Cornell University Press.

MATERA, F. J. 1987 *What Are They Saying about Mark?* New York/Mahwah: Paulist Press.

McKEE, J. 1974 *Literary Irony and the Literary Audience: Studies in the Victimization of the Reader in Augustan Fiction*. Amsterdam: Ropodi.

MEHTONEN, P. 1993 'Poetiikka – tieteellistä järjestystä taiteen epäjärjestykseen?' P. Ahokas and L. Rojola (eds), *Toiseuden politiikat*. Yearbook of the Literary Research Society 47. Helsinki: Finnish Literature Society.

—— 1996 *Old Concepts and New Poetics:* Historia, Argumentum, *and* Fabula *in the Twelfth- and Early Thirteenth-Century Latin Poetics of Fiction*. Commentationes Humanarum Litterarum 108. Helsinki: Societas Scientiarum Fennica.

MERENLAHTI, P. and HAKOLA, R. 1999 'Reconceiving Narrative Criticism.' D. Rhoads and K. Syreeni (eds), *Characterization in the Gospels: Reconceiving Narrative Criticism*. JSNTSup 184. Sheffield: Sheffield Academic Press.

MINER, E. R. 1990 *Comparative Poetics: An Intercultural Essay on Theories of Literature*. Princeton: Princeton University Press.

MOORE, S. D. 1987 'Are the Gospels Unified Narratives?' SBLSP.

—— 1989 *Literary Criticism and the Gospels: The Theoretical Challenge*. New Haven: Yale University Press.

—— 1992 *Mark and Luke in Poststructuralist Perspectives: Jesus Begins to Write*. New Haven: Yale University Press.

—— 1994 *Poststructuralism and the New Testament: Derrida and Foucault at the Foot of the Cross*. Minneapolis: Fortress Press.

NEIRYNCK, F. 1988 *Duality in Mark: Contributions to the Study of the Markan Redaction.* Revised Edition with Supplementary Notes. BETL XXXI. Leuven: Leuven University Press.

NORTON, D. 1993a *A History of the Bible as Literature. Volume One: From antiquity to 1700.* Cambridge: Cambridge University Press.

—— 1993b *A History of the Bible as Literature. Volume Two: From 1700 to the present day.* Cambridge: Cambridge University Press.

NOTH, M. 1981 (1943) *The Deuteronomistic history.* JSOTSup 15. Sheffield: JSOT Press.

VAN OYEN, G. 1992 'Intercalation and Irony in the Gospel of Mark.' F. van Segbroeck, C. M. Tuckett, C. van Belle and J. Verheyden (eds), *The Four Gospels 1992* (FS Fr. Neirynck). BETL C. Leuven: Leuven University Press.

PELLING, C. (ed.) 1990 *Characterization and Individuality in Greek Literature.* Oxford: Clarendon Press.

PERRIN, N. 1976 'The Interpretation of the Gospel of Mark.' *Int* 30.

PERRY, M. and STERNBERG, M. 1986 (1968) 'The King Through Ironic Eyes: Biblical Narrative and the Literary Reading Process.' *Poetics Today* 7:2.

PETERSEN, N. R. 1974 'On the Notion of Genre.' *Semeia* 1.

—— 1978a '"Point of View" in Mark's Narrative.' *Semeia* 12.

—— 1978b *Literary Criticism for New Testament Critics.* Philadelphia: Fortress Press.

—— 1994 'Can One Speak of a Gospel Genre?' *Neot* 28.

PHELAN, J. 1996 *Narrative as Rhetoric: Technique, Audiences, Ethics, Ideology.* Columbus: Ohio State University Press.

PORTER, S. E. 1995 'Literary Approaches to the New Testament: From Formalism to Deconstruction and Back.' S. Porter and D. Tombs (eds), *Approaches to New Testament Study.* Sheffield: Sheffield Academic Press.

POWELL, M. A. 1990 *What is Narrative Criticism?* Minneapolis: Fortress Press.

—— 2001 *Chasing the Eastern Star: Adventures in Biblical Reader-Response Criticism.* Louisville: Westminster John Knox Press.

PRINCE, G. 1982 *Narratology: The Form and Function of Narrative.* Berlin: Mouton.

PRINCE, G. 1987 *A Dictionary of Narratology.* Lincoln and London: University of Nebraska Press.

PROPP, V. 1958 (1928) *Morphology of the Folktale.* Trans. L. Scott. Bloomington: Indiana University Press.

RABINOWITZ, P. J. 1987 *Before Reading: Narrative Conventions and the Politics of Interpretation.* Ithaca and London: Cornell University Press.

RÄISÄNEN, H. 1983 'The Messianic Secret in Mark's Gospel.' C. Tuckett (ed.), *The Messianic Secret.* Philadelphia: Fortress Press.

—— 1987 *Paul and the Law.* 2nd edn. WUNT 29. Tübingen: Mohr (Siebeck).

—— 1990 *The 'Messianic Secret' in Mark.* Trans. C. Tuckett. Edinburgh: T&T Clark.

—— 1995 'The New Testament in Theology.' P. Byrne and L. Houlden (eds), *Companion Encyclopaedia of Theology.* London and New York: Routledge.

REED, W. L. 1993 *Dialogues of the Word: The Bible as Literature According to Bakhtin.* New York: Oxford University Press.

REINHARTZ, A. 1988 'The New Testament and anti-Judaism: A Literary-Critical Approach.' *JES* 25.

RHOADS, D. M. 1982 'Narrative Criticism and the Gospel of Mark.' *JAAR* 50.

—— 1993 'Losing Life for Others in the Face of Death: Mark's Standards of Judgment.' *Int* 47.

—— 1994 'Jesus and the Syrophoenician Woman in Mark. A Narrative-Critical Study.' *JAAR* 62.

—— 1999 'Narrative Criticism: Practices and Prospects.' D. Rhoads and K. Syreeni (eds), *Characterization in the Gospels: Reconceiving Narrative Criticism.* JSNTSup 184. Sheffield: Sheffield Academic Press.

RHOADS, D. M. and MICHIE, D. 1982 *Mark as Story: An Introduction to the Narrative of a Gospel.* Philadelphia: Fortress Press.

RICHARDSON, W. J. 1983 'Lacan and the Subject of Psychoanalysis.' J. H. Smith and W. Kerrigan (eds), *Interpreting Lacan.* Psychiatry and the Humanities 6. New Haven: Yale University Press.

RICKARD, J. S. 1994 'Introduction.' P. Brooks, *Psychoanalysis and Story-telling.* Oxford: Blackwell.

RICOEUR, P. 1984 *Time and Narrative.* Vol. 1. Trans. K. McLaughlin and D. Pellauer. Chicago: University of Chicago Press.

RICOEUR, P. 1990 'Interpretative Narrative.' R. M. Schwartz (ed.), *The Book and the Text: The Bible and Literary Theory*. Cambridge and Oxford: Basil Blackwell.

RIMMON-KENAN, S. 1983 *Narrative Fiction: Contemporary Poetics*. New York: Methuen.

ROBBINS, V. K. 1992 *Jesus the Teacher: A Socio-Rhetorical Interpretation of Mark. Paperback edition with new introduction and additional indexes*. Minneapolis: Fortress Press.

—— 1996a *The Tapestry of Early Christian Discourse: Rhetoric, Society, and Ideology*. New York: Routledge.

—— 1996b *Exploring the Texture of Texts: A Guide to Socio-Rhetorical Interpretation*. Valley Forge: Trinity Press International.

ROBINSON, J. M. 1965 'The Problem of history in Mark, reconsidered.' *USQR* 20.

—— 1970 'On the Gattung of Mark (and John).' *Jesus and Man's Hope*. Vol. I. Pittsburgh: Pittsburgh Theological Seminary.

—— 1978 'Gnosticism and the New Testament.' *Gnosis: Festschrift für Hans Jonas*. Göttingen: Vandenhoeck & Ruprecht.

—— 1986 'The Gospels as Narrative.' F. McConnell (ed.), *The Bible and the Narrative Tradition*. New York: Oxford University Press.

ROBINSON, J. M. and KOESTER, H. 1971 *Trajectories through Early Christianity*. Philadelphia: Fortress Press.

DE SAUSSURE, F. 1977 (1915) *Course in General Linguistics*. (Ed.) C. Bally and A. Sechehaye. London: Fontana/Collins.

SCHOTTROFF, L. and STEGEMANN, W. 1986 (1978) *Jesus and the Hope of the Poor*. Maryknoll: Orbis.

SCHULZ, S. 1972 *Q – die Spruchquelle der Evangelisten*. Zürich: Theologischer Verlag Zürich.

SCHWALL, H. 1997 'Lacan and the Bible.' *Literature & Theology* 11.

SCHWEIZER, E. 1985 'Mark's Theological Achievement.' W. Telford (ed.), *The Interpretation of Mark*. IRT 7. London: SPCK.

SECCOMBE, D. 1982 *Possessions and the Poor in Luke-Acts*. Studien zum Neuen Testament und Seiner Umwelt B/6. Linz.

SEELEY, D. 1994 *Deconstructing the New Testament*. Biblical Interpretation 5. Leiden: E. J. Brill.

SHINER, W. T. 1995 *Follow Me! Disciples in Markan Rhetoric*. SBLDS 145. Atlanta: Scholars Press.

STALEY, J. L. 1988 *The Print's First Kiss: A Rhetorical Investigation of the Implied Reader in the Fourth Gospel.* SBLDS 82. Atlanta: Scholars Press.

—— 1993 'Subversive Narrator/Victimized Reader. A Reader Response Assessment of a Text-Critical Problem, John 18.12–24.' *JSNT* 51.

—— 1999 *Reading with a Passion: Rhetoric, Autobiography, and the American West in the Gospel of John.* New York: Continuum.

STANZEL, F. 1986 (1979) *A Theory of Narrative.* Trans. C. Goedsche. Cambridge: Cambridge University Press.

STECK, O. H. 1967 *Israel und das Gewaltsame Geschick der Propheten. Untersuchungen zur Überlieferung des deuteronomistischen Geschichtbildes im Alten Testament, Spätjudentum und Urchristentum.* WMANT 23. Neukirchen-Vluyn: Neukirchener Verlag.

STEINER, G. 1989 *Real Presences.* Chicago: The University of Chicago Press.

STENDAHL, K. 1968 *The School of St. Matthew.* 2nd edn. Philadelphia: Fortress Press.

STERNBERG, M. 1985 *Poetics of Biblical Narrative: Ideological Literature and the Drama of Reading.* Bloomington: Indiana University Press.

SWINGEWOOD, A. 1986 *Sociological Poetics and Aesthetic Theory.* London: Macmillan.

SYREENI, K. 1988 'Jeesuksen 'läsnäolo' evankeliumeissa.' R. Saarinen and R. Uro (eds), *Lopun ajat ennen ja nyt.* Kirkon tutkimuskeskus A 48. Pieksämäki.

—— 1990a 'Matthew, Luke, and the Law: A Study in Hermeneutical Exegesis.' T. Veijola (ed.), *The Law in the Bible and in its Environment.* Publications of the Finnish Exegetical Society 51. Helsinki: The Finnish Exegetical Society/Göttingen: Vandenhoek & Ruprecht.

—— 1990b, 'Between Heaven and Earth: On the Structure of Matthew's Symbolic Universe.' *JSNT* 40.

—— 1991 'The Gospel in Paradigms: A Study in the Hermeneutical Space of Luke-Acts.' P. Luomanen (ed.), *Luke-Acts: Scandinavian Perspectives.* Publications of the Finnish Exegetical Society 54. Helsinki: The Finnish Exegetical Society/Göttingen: Vandenhoek & Ruprecht.

—— 1994 'Separation and Identity: Aspects of the Symbolic World of Matt 6.1–18.' *NTS* 40.

—— 1995 'Metaphorical Appropriation: (Post-)Modern Biblical Hermeneutics and the Theory of Metaphor.' *Literature and Theology* 9.

SYREENI, K. 1997 'Tre världar: En inledning till den hermeneutiska trevärlds-modellen.' *Religion och Bibel* 56.

—— 1999 'Peter as Character and Symbol in the Gospel of Matthew.' D. Rhoads and K. Syreeni (eds), *Characterization in the Gospels: Reconceiving Narrative Criticism.* JSNTSup 184. Sheffield: Sheffield Academic Press.

TAMMI, P. 1992 *Kertova teksti. Esseitä narratologiasta.* Jyväskylä: Gaudeamus.

—— 1995 'Uutinen ja fiktio. Kaksi metakriittistä huomautusta narratologian soveltamisesta journalistisiin teksteihin.' *Proosan taiteesta. Leevi Valkaman juhlakirja.* Turun yliopisto, Taiteiden tutkimuksen laitos: Sarja A, n:o 32, yleinen kirjallisuustiede.

TANNEHILL, R. C. 1977 'The Disciples in Mark: the Function of a Narrative Role.' *JR* 57.

—— 1979 'The Gospel of Mark as Narrative Christology.' *Semeia* 16.

TATE, W. R. 1997 *Biblical Interpretation: An Integrated Approach.* Revised Edition. Peabody: Hendrickson Publishers.

TELFORD, W. R. 1980 *The Barren Temple and The Withered Tree: a Redaction-Critical Analysis of the Cursing of the Fig-tree Pericope in Mark's Gospel and Its Relation to the Cleansing of the Temple Tradition.* JSNTSup 1. Sheffield: JSOT Press.

THEISSEN, G. 1973 'Wanderradikalismus. Literatursoziologische Aspekte der Überlieferung von Worten Jesu im Urchristentum.' *ZTK* 70.

—— 1983 (1974) *The Miracle Stories of the Early Christian Tradition.* Trans. F. McDonagh. Philadelphia: Fortress Press.

—— 1987 (1983) *Psychological Aspects of Pauline Theology.* Trans. J. P. Galvin. Philadelphia: Fortress Press.

THOMPSON, J. B. 1990 *Ideology and Modern Culture: Critical Social Theory in the Era of Mass Communication.* Cambridge: Polity Press.

TODOROV, T. 1969 *Grammaire du 'Décaméron.'* The Hague: Mouton.

—— 1988 *Literature and Its Theorists: A Personal View of Twentieth-Century Criticism.* Trans. C. Porter. London: Routledge & Kegan Paul.

TOKER, L. 1993 *Eloquent Reticence: Withholding Information in Fictional Narrative.* Lexington: University Press of Kentucky.

TOLBERT, M. A. 1989 *Sowing the Gospel: Mark's World in Literary-Historical Perspective.* Minneapolis: Fortress Press.

TOLBERT, M. A. 1990 'The Gospel in Greco-Roman Culture.' R. M. Schwartz (ed.), *The Book and the Text: The Bible and Literary Theory.* Cambridge: Basil Blackwell.

—— 1993 'How the Gospel of Mark Builds Character.' *Int* 47.

TRILLING, L. 1961 'Freud and Literature.' *The Liberal Imagination.* London: Mercury. (First published in 1951.)

VISOTZKY, B. L. 1996 *Reading the Book: Making the Bible a Timeless Text.* New York: Schocken Books. (Originally published by Anchor Books, Doubleday, New York in 1991.)

WALASKAY, P. 1983 *'And so we came to Rome.'* *The Political Perspective of St. Luke.* SNTSMS 49. Cambridge: Cambridge University Press.

WALTON, K. L. 1990 *Mimesis as Make-Believe: On Foundations of the Representational Arts.* Cambridge: Harvard University Press.

WILDE, J. A. 1978 'The Social World of Mark's Gospel: A Word about Method.' SBLSP.

WILSON, B. R. 1963 'A Typology of Sects in a Dynamic and Comparative Perspective.' *Archives de Sociologie de Religion* 16.

—— 1969 'A Typology of Sects.' R. Robertson (ed.), *Sociology of Religion.* Baltimore: Penguin Books.

—— 1973 *Magic and the Millennium: A Sociological Study of Religious Movements of Protest among Tribal and Third-World Peoples.* New York: Harper & Row.

WREDE, W. 1901 *Das Messiasgeheimnis in den Evangelien: Zugleich ein Beitrag zum Verständnis des Markusevangeliums.* Göttingen: Vandenhoeck & Ruprecht.

—— 1904 'Zur Heilung des Gelähmten (Mc 2,1ff.).' *ZNW* 5.

WRIGHT, E. 1984 *Psychoanalytic Criticism: Theory in Practice.* London: Methuen.

Index of Names

Index of Readings

Index of Subjects

actantial roles 86

Acts of the Apostles 2, 10, 23, 51–3, 54, 69, 87, 95, 104, 109, 124, 141

    Ethiopian eunuch in 51–3, 141

    see also Luke's gospel/Luke–Acts

allegorical interpretation 48, 49, 130, 145

    see also 'deep' ('close') reading, in relation to gospels

ambiguity 28, 40–2, 44, 61–76, 80–1, 110–11

Anatomy of the Fourth Gospel: A Study in Literary Design (Culpepper, 1983) 21, 22, 23, 54

anti-Semitism 11, 122–3

aretalogical composition, Mark as 107

assumption of unity, within narrative criticism 24–5

    see also narrative unity

authoritative (monologic) discourse 33, 75–6, 92–7

Bathsheba, story of 61–3

betrayal, of Jesus 86–8

canon, literary 2–3, 4, 20, 28, 32–3, 34, 50, 63, 116

'carnal' (literal) reading, in relation to gospels 46–55, 141

The Carpenter (Ågren, 1996) 36, 42

characterization, biblical 13, 22, 23, 39, 49, 52, 54, 61–2, 70–1, 74, 77–97, 108, 122

'close' ('deep') reading, in relation to gospels 46–58, 108–9, 141

    see also allegorical interpretation

code, narrative as 55

coherence *see* narrative unity

common (ordinary), place of in Mark's gospel 38–40

concealment and disclosure, as elements of plot in gospels 108–10

conscious, the, in relation to the unconscious 139, 140–1

conservatism, political, in relation to New Criticism 56

conservative theology, in relation to narrative criticism 56–7

contestatory symbolic forms 93–8

control, over reader through narrative rhetoric 25–6, 33, 52, 70–1, 72

'creativity debate', concerning Mark's gospel 20–1, 23

culture

    of affirmation 93

    of contestation 93–8

    cultural studies 7, 116

    in relation to poetics, overview 1–9

David and Bathsheba, story of 61–3

death

    and resurrection of Jesus *see* passion, of Jesus

    instinct in relation to narrative 132–3

deconstruction, literary 3, 29, 34, 44, 121–2, 128, 137, 144–5

'deep' ('close') reading, in relation to gospels 46–58, 108–9, 141

    see also allegorical interpretation

déjà-lu 53

deliberate interpretive fictions (instrumental metaphors)

    see metaphoric language; truth fictions

'desolating sacrilege' 71–2

Deuteronomist theology 137–8

Mark's gospel
  as aretalogical compoosition 107
  characterization in 79, 82–7, 89–96
  disciples in 41, 47, 50, 53, 64, 69, 82,
    83, 84, 85, 102, 103, 109
  ending of 41–2, 110
  implied reader, in relation to 46–8,
    50–1, 57–8
  literary nature of 6, 35–44, 110–11
  miracle stories in 37, 106
  mixing of styles in 38–40
  'modernism' of 40–2
  narrative rhetoric of, gaps and
    ambiguity in 61–76
  narrative unity of 17–18, 19, 20–3,
    32, 36–7
  parables in see Markan Parable Theory
  plot of 39, 103, 106–7, 108, 109,
    110–11
  'realism' of 38–40
  receptions of 35–44
  secrecy motif 41, 61, 64, 73, 75, 102,
    106, 107, 109
  standards of judgment 57–8, 89
  theatre performances of 36
Markan Parable Theory 50–1, 53, 63–4,
    108, 141
  see also parabolic teaching
Markan 'sandwiches' 66–7
Marxist criticism 3, 4, 5, 56, 93
Matthew's gospel
  as a manual of discipline 95, 109
  characterization of Jewish leaders
    in 122–3
  narrative unity of 19, 31
  in relation to Mark 36–7, 43, 64, 68,
    71, 77, 87, 92, 94, 108, 109
mediation, text as relationship of 118,
    124, 128
Mediterranean world 124, 125–6
Messianic secret see secrecy motif
metaphoric language 14, 84, 110–11,
    129–30, 131–42, 143–6
metonymy, Mark's open ending as 110
midrash 46, 130
mimesis, concept of 4, 9–10, 38–40,
    121, 124, 125
Mimesis: The Representation of Reality in
    Western Literature (Auerbach,
    1946) 39–40, 63, 79, 80, 85, 92

miracle stories in Mark see Mark's gospel
mixing of styles, in Mark's gospel 38–40
modernism
  of Mark's gospel 40–2
  in relation to politics of art 56
  see also postmodernism
monologic (authoritative) discourse 33,
    75–6, 92–7
  see also narrative unity

Nag Hammadi Library 43
narrateme 48
narrative christologies, gospels as 8,
    109
'Narrative Criticism and the Gospel of
    Mark' (Rhoads, 1982) 9, 17–18,
    69, 115, 117
'Narrative Criticism: Practices and
    Prospects' (Rhoads, 1999) 115–18
narrative gaps 24, 52–3, 61–76, 80–1
narrative kerygma 8, 64, 104–5
narrative rhetoric 13, 18, 25, 27, 61–76,
    122
  see also control; direction, indirection
narrative subjectivity 88–97
narrative unity
  of gospels, debate concerning 17–34,
    75, 76, 97, 116
  as measure of literary value in
    traditional Western literary
    paradigm 2–3
  in relation to ego-psychological
    criticism 135–8
narratology 9, 12, 17, 18, 19, 21, 22–3,
    25, 28–9, 35, 57, 61, 89, 125, 126,
    134
narrator, role of 10–11, 13, 22, 25–7,
    52, 61–3, 66, 67, 68–75, 83–4,
    122–3
  see also unreliable narrator
neurosis 132
New Criticism 19–20, 56–7
'new historicism' 7, 118
Nicodemus 54
non-fiction (factual), in relation to
    fiction 9–12, 119, 123

objective poetics, search for 3–4
Old Testament prophecy, interpretation
    of 51–3, 87